WITHDRAWN
FROM THE RECORDS OF THE
MID-CONTINENT PUBLIC LIBRARY

COVENTRY
MURDERS

COVENTRY
MURDERS

VANESSA MORGAN

First published 2014

The History Press
The Mill, Brimscombe Port
Stroud, Gloucestershire, GL5 2QG
www.thehistorypress.co.uk

© Vanessa Morgan, 2014

The right of Vanessa Morgan to be identified as the Author
of this work has been asserted in accordance with the
Copyright, Designs and Patents Act 1988.

All rights reserved. No part of this book may be reprinted
or reproduced or utilised in any form or by any electronic,
mechanical or other means, now known or hereafter invented,
including photocopying and recording, or in any information
storage or retrieval system, without the permission in writing
from the Publishers.

British Library Cataloguing in Publication Data.
A catalogue record for this book is available from the British Library.

ISBN 978 0 7509 5221 7

Typesetting and origination by The History Press
Printed in Great Britain

CONTENTS

ACKNOWLEDGEMENTS

Research for this book was mainly undertaken using local newspapers of the period, including the *Coventry Herald*, the *Coventry Times*, the *Coventry Mercury*, the *Coventry Evening Telegraph*, the *Leamington Spa Courier*, the *Birmingham Gazette*, the *Birmingham Journal* and the *Birmingham Daily Post*, all of which are held at either the Coventry History Centre, the Warwick Record Office or the Library of Birmingham. Other original registers and census records are sourced from the Warwick Record Office.

All images, unless otherwise stated, are from the author's collections of original photographs, old postcards or newspaper cuttings.

Market Square *c.* 1910, a prominent historic site. The prestigious Leofric Hotel was built here in the 1950s. Plans are now being made to turn the building into student flats.

INTRODUCTION

On the night of 14 November 1940 the skies above Coventry were ablaze. For miles around the horizon was lit up like a brilliant but devastating sunset. Everyone in those neighbouring towns had one thing on their lips – 'Coventry's getting it tonight.'

Over the course of around ten hours, 400 bombers from the German Luftwaffe dropped their bombs upon the city until, by dawn the next morning, Coventry was a mass of rubble. A great number of buildings were destroyed, including the fourteenth-century cathedral, St Michael's. It had only become a cathedral twenty years earlier in 1919 although previously it had been described as one of the largest parish churches in the country. Therefore, when Coventry became a diocese, St Michael's became its cathedral. Now, sadly, all that was left of it was the tower, spire and

The ruined outer walls of Coventry Cathedral, 2013.

outer walls. The people of Coventry were in a state of shock and for once it was being reported that the British Bulldog spirit had crumbled.

The rebuilding of Coventry began in 1948 with Princess Elizabeth laying the foundation stone for a new cathedral which was built at the side of the ruins of St Michael's. It was consecrated in 1962 in the presence Elizabeth, now queen, and also named St Michael's.

This period of Coventry's history is probably one which the city of Coventry is most associated with. Another concerns the wife

The outer wall of the new cathedral, 2013.

A statue of Lady Godiva, unveiled in 1949, stands in Broadgate, 2013.

of Leofric, Earl of Mercia and Lord of Coventry. Under Leofric's rule in the eleventh century, the people of Coventry were heavily taxed. Legend has it that his wife, Lady Godiva, pleaded with him to lift the excessive taxes and her husband, tired of her persistence, told her that if she rode naked through the streets of Coventry he would do as she asked. At this Godiva asked the people of Coventry to close their shutters and bolt their doors and, letting down her long fair hair to fall as a cloak, she did as her husband asked.

Only one man, a tailor called Tom, disobeyed her order and opened his shutters just enough to see her ride past. As a result he was immediately struck blind. Whether this is fable or fact no one really knows but everyone has heard of Lady Godiva, and 'peeping Tom' has become a common expression.

Being 'sent to Coventry' is another saying associated with this town and there are many myths about how this idiom came about. A popular one comes from the era of the Civil War, during a time when Oliver Cromwell sent many Scottish Royalist prisoners to be housed in St John's church. They were allowed to walk around the streets for exercise but, being a staunchly Parliamentarian city, the people avoided them and young girls were told not to speak to them. This isolation and antipathy meant that many soldiers were unhappy about the idea of being sent to Coventry.

A different meaning could be taken from the sixteenth-century heretics who were brought to Coventry to be burned. Again, Coventry was not a place you would have wanted to have been sent to in those times.

The population of Coventry at the time of Lady Godiva was about 350. By the fourteenth century this figure had risen to nearly 5,000 which, by the standards of those days, made it a considerably large town. When the first census was taken in 1801 the population was 16,000 but by 1851 that figure had risen to 37,000 and by 1900 to 62,000.

For 400 years Coventry enjoyed the exulted status of being a county. During the War of the Roses, the Lancastrian king, Henry VI, had sheltered in Coventry during his campaign and, in 1451, he gave the city the title County of the City of Coventry. This status was taken away during the 1840s following the Boundary Act of 1842 and Coventry became part of Warwickshire.

In the Middle Ages, Coventry was prospering due to its wool industry, predominantly through the weaving and dying of wool. It was here, in this industry, that another saying was popularised – 'true blue'. The Coventry dyers were well known for producing a blue cloth that did not fade and remained colour-fast in washing, and 'as true as Coventry blue' soon became a popular phrase when implying something was long-lasting and enduring.

By the eighteenth century the woollen industry was beginning to decline, although the employment of silk-ribbon weaving was rapidly expanding. This trend continued until the 1860s when a treaty was made with France in 1860 which allowed free trade. Silk ribbons flooded into England from France and the Coventry workers faced ruin. However, while the ribbon makers in Coventry were facing ruin, the watchmaking industry was flourishing. The first watchmakers were found in Coventry in the eighteenth century, even as early as the late seventeenth century, but it was in the late nineteenth century that watchmaking in Coventry was at its height. Bicycles were also manufactured in Coventry at this time. The first bicycles in Britain were made here in the 1860s and, as cycling became more popular, this industry also began to expand in the town. Towards the end of the century, in 1897, Coventry businesses were producing the first cars to be manufactured in the city.

Like other towns in the nineteenth century, Coventry prospered by the development of these new industries and inventions. A gasworks was opened in 1820 and the streets were given gas lighting. The railways arrived in 1838 and a hospital was also built in 1838. The cemetery was created in 1847 and, due to a smallpox epidemic in 1871, a fever hospital was opened in 1874. A sewage system was developed in the late nineteenth century and electricity arrived in 1895. Steam trams travelled the streets in 1884 and they were replaced by their electric counterparts in 1895.

Before the nineteenth century the town was policed in the old manorial way. Then in the early 1800s watchmen and special constables were employed to police the streets with the senior officer, known as the High Constable, being elected annually. Thomas Henry Prosser, who had previously been a Bow Street Runner, was elected in 1832.

The Municipal Corporation Act in 1836 reformed this old system. Boroughs throughout England were required to organise police forces; so Coventry enrolled a police inspector, a sergeant and twenty constables.

A busy Broadgate *c.* 1950, with buses, cars and electric trams.

Thomas Prosser was then appointed as chief superintendent. This new force began operating on 7 March 1836 but for a while surrounding villages, such as Berkeswell, continued with the old system.

It seems this new force was supervised with great care and efficiency as, according to the *Coventry Times* on 7 April 1858 when Thomas Prosser retired in that year, the force presented him with a bronze clock inscribed with the words 'Presented by the officers and men of the Coventry Police to Mr Thomas Henry Prosser as a testimonial of respect and esteem for his uniform kindness and upright conduct towards them during the twenty-one years he held the office of their Chief Superintendent.'

The old courthouse and gaol, County Hall, opened in 1783 and remained open until the late 1980s. Then it lay derelict on the corner of Bayley Lane and Cuckoo Lane until May 2012 when it opened as a bar called The Establishment. The building retains an ambiance of how it used to be, with the judge's seat, the crest, the public gallery and the dock still in evidence. The cells have been made into dining areas and even the old keys to lock up the inmates are on display.

The old court house, 2013.

Inside the old court house, now a bar and grill, 2013.

The dining area leading to the cells, 2013.

The keys to the cell doors, now on display, 2013.

The prison governor's house, on the corner of Bayley Lane and Cuckoo Lane, 2013.

The prison governor's house was built on the side of the County Hall in Pepper Lane.

In the 1840s, when reverted back to being part of Warwickshire, the Coventry Assizes were abolished and those cases which needed to be tried by an assize judge were transferred to Warwick.

Up until 1831, public hangings took place at Whitley Common and then outside County Hall. When the assizes were transferred to Warwick they then took place outside Warwick Goal. Public hangings were considered a day out for most people and thousands would gather, often a few hours before the execution was due to take place in order to get a good view. There they would remain, watching the body hanging for the usual time of one hour, in order to see it being taken down. A number of the accused would also be sentenced to be dissected after their execution and people were keen to attended public dissections as well, with large numbers turning up to view the internal organs of the criminal.

Dissection was used as an additional punishment for the worst offenders through to the first half of the nineteenth century. Christians believed a person could only be resurrected on Judgement Day if a body was complete, therefore, dismemberment was considered a fitting punishment for those worst offenders. The body would be publically dissected and then exhibited and any family member trying to rescue the body prior to this fate would face a ten-year transportation. This form of punishment replaced the practise of hanging, drawing and quartering criminals, with the four parts of the body placed on stakes around a town as a gruesome deterrent. Dissection also assisted anatomists and medical students in their studies as, in those times, these were the only bodies available.

In July 1832 a bill went through parliament abolishing dissection. Lord Wynford, the deputy speaker for the House of Lords, was against this, protesting that he had known instances when the dread of dissection had produced more fear than death itself. Nevertheless, the bill was passed and Lord Grey suggested that the bodies of those executed would be buried beneath the gallows or in the confines of the gaol without funeral rites. This was also passed. As the years progressed graves were reopened and several would be buried in one grave.

Another custom of the time was to take a death mask of the hanged person. This was in order to answer the question – was it possible to tell from the shape of the head whether someone could be the type of person to commit murder?

The next reform in execution came in 1868. At the time of Kington's execution in 1859 (detailed in case number five) the newspapers were reporting that there was already a change in the public excitement surrounding execution. The *Leamington Spa Courier* on 31 December wrote that public opinion seemed to be changing regarding the viewing of an execution:

> There is something too mysterious and solemn about death for any man, however depraved, to look upon it. When society, as a vindication of an outrage upon its law, assumes the awful and responsible power of depriving a fellow creature of his life, and in order that that solemn act shall lose none of its effect, as a terror to the evil doer, and a warning to those whose ungovernable passion becomes a frenzy, takes care, that he who has to pay the penalty of this outrage, by the forfeiture of his life, shall pass from life unto death, on the public scaffold, it assumes a prerogative which gives to all men an instinctive shudder, and which no person with a well constituted mind voluntarily witnesses.

Although the reporter for this newspaper conveys the idea that people were losing interest in hangings, a letter published in the *Coventry Herald* on 14 January 1860 seemed to disagree. The writer notes: 'An execution is witnessed by two hundred, three hundred or a thousand persons; whilst as execution reported by the representatives of the press is conveyed to millions, both abroad and at home.' People were, it seems, still willing to voluntarily witness, or read about, execution.

Nonetheless, an act in 1868 abolished public hanging and executions now took place within the confines of the gaol. For a while reporters were allowed to witness the execution for the benefit of describing the scene to the public as they (the public) the press said, 'demand to be informed of all reasonable details in connexion with so unusual an event'.

Coventry *c.* 1850, showing the three spires looking north from Warwick Road.

Even when there was no execution to watch certain people would still gather outside the gaol to watch the blag flag being hoisted showing that the execution was taking place. In 1902 this practise also ended as it was felt that this 'often aroused interest in minds of morbidly inclined people to assemble outside the prison'. Even the prison chaplain, instead of reciting the service for burial while the man was still alive, now waited until the executioner had done his job and the prisoner was dead.

In the late seventeenth century a travel writer described Coventry as standing on the side of a pretty hill. The spire and steeple of one of its churches was very high, thought to be the third highest in England and, with all the other towers from neighbouring churches and high buildings standing close by, the town looked very impressive. With its broad streets being well paved with small stones, Coventry was an ideal place to visit. But lurking behind this facade grisly murders were about to take place, some of which are now chronicled in the following pages.

Vanessa Morgan, 2014

CASE ONE 1831

HIS WICKED NIECE

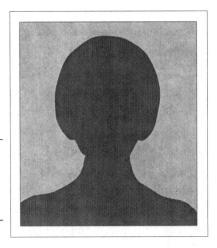

Suspect: Mary Ann Higgins

Age: 20

Charge: Murder

A labouring man, named William Higgins, residing in Spon Street, in this City, having died suddenly on Tuesday night last, an opinion was formed that he had been poisoned. After a diligent enquiry, on the part of Mr Barton, chief constable, and others, suspicion fell upon a young girl named Mary Ann Higgins, a niece of the deceased, who resided with him. She was accordingly taken into custody on Wednesday night, by Gardner, constable, and conveyed to the Watch House

Leamington Spa Courier, 26 March 1831

Mary Ann Higgins was born in Henley in Arden, Warwickshire, in 1811. It seems either her parents couldn't look after her or they didn't want to because, at the age of 12 months, her grandparents took her to live with them somewhere near Coventry. When they died her mother still wouldn't have her back so she went to live with an aunt in Manchester. This was probably around January 1826 as two burials are recorded in the registers of the parish for Wooton Wawen and Henley in Arden for that year. One was a Samuel Higgins, who was buried on 2 January 1826. He was aged 65 and from Coventry. The other is for an Elizabeth Higgins from Coventry who was buried on 14 January 1826, aged 62.

How happy Mary was at being sent to her aunt is not known but it is clear that the aunt kept a house of ill-repute and, by the age of 14, Mary had become a prostitute. People described Mary as a good-looking girl with a fresh colour and clear complexion, but said she didn't have an 'intellectual appearance'.

Mary did eventually leave her aunt's house and go into service but her love of nice dresses led her into a life of crime. At one point it was recorded she was on the brink of being transported. It was then that her uncle stepped in and she went back to Coventry to live with him at his house in Spon Street.

Her Uncle William was unmarried and looked after Mary as if she was his own child. He was said to be of 'humble station', but it seems he had saved a reasonable amount of money for those times, which he had invested and was earning interest from. Some said it was about £100 and that he was also known to have a collection of guinea coins in the house. All this he intended to leave to Mary when he died.

Sometime around the Christmas of 1830 Mary met Edward Clarke; a young man who was an apprentice at Vale and Co., a watch factory in Coventry. At the age of 21 he would appear to have been an ideal suitor

Spon Street today. A mixture of the old and new.

for the young girl; perhaps her uncle thought so too as he certainly seemed to encourage the match. However, by February it was noticed that Edward seemed to be in possession of more money than usual. He also had one or two guinea coins, just like those which William Higgins had in his house. Edward would quite often boast, 'I have only to go to the old man's house whenever I want money.'

On 22 March 1831 Mary went into a local shop and asked for 2d worth of arsenic saying she wanted to get rid of some rats. As was the law in those days the shop assistant refused to sell her any unless she had a witness with her. Perhaps in the hope that someone would ignore the law she went to another shop but again was given the same answer. In Spon Street Mary met up with a girl she knew called Elizabeth Russell. Elizabeth was on her way to Vale and Co. and Mary said she would accompany her but needed to buy some arsenic first. So together they went into Messrs Wyley and again Mary explained she wanted to 'destroy some rats'. This time she was successful in her purchase and, after paying for it, asked the shopkeeper how to use it. She was told to mix it with some bread or something similar. The arsenic was then wrapped in a paper bag with a label 'arsenic, poison' attached to it and given to Mary. As she left the shop she tore off the label saying, 'What has he stuck this on for?'

The two girls then headed for the factory. It was now one o'clock and the men were leaving for dinner. Mary met Edward and, leaving Elizabeth, they went back to her uncle's house.

At two o'clock Edward returned to the factory and stayed there until eight in the evening. From there he went straight back to the Higgin's house where he spent the rest of the evening. Later that evening he was seen outside in the yard with William Higgins, where William appeared to be being sick.

A few hours later, at one o'clock in the morning, Mrs Green, a neighbour, was awoken by someone banging on her door. It was Mary, who seemed to be very distressed and begged Mrs Green to go back to her uncle's with her as he was very ill. Mrs Green found William lying across Mary's bed. When she felt him he appeared stiff but she thought he was still breathing. She noticed there was some liquid on the floor so, realising that he had been sick, Mrs Green went to make him some tea. While doing so she heard Mary cry out, 'Oh I hear my uncle groan,' and when she went back

Part of the building which was once Vale & Co., founded 1750, still standing in Spon Street today.

found that William was dead. Mary was crying, 'Oh my dear uncle! Oh my dear uncle! Now he's gone, all my friends are gone.'

Mary said they had had pea soup for supper and, just afterwards, her uncle had felt ill and had gone to bed. Later, however, he had come to her room saying he felt really sick so she had put him in her bed while she went for help.

Mary then said that she was supposed to be getting married on Easter Monday and that she was 'in the family way' so could not delay; although it wouldn't be the same without her uncle. She said she would put off the mourning for that one day because it was supposed to be unlucky to be married in black, and that she would go back to it afterwards. This story later proved to be untrue. Mary wasn't expecting a baby or getting married.

In the morning another neighbour, Mrs Moore, came to enquire if it was true that William had died. Mary said yes and she was just going out for some mourning clothes. Noticing that the place looked untidy Mrs Moore offered to help Mary by tidying up while she was out. Mary agreed and this was the mistake which was going to condemn her.

In the kitchen Mrs Moore saw two basins of pea soup. One appeared very different from a usual pea soup, being whitish in colour and thicker in consistency; the other was quite normal. She left them on one side and asked Mary about it when she returned. Mary said that one had been thickened with flour, the other with oatmeal.

Mrs Moore, however, was unconvinced and gave the suspicious-looking soup to the carpenter who had come to measure for the coffin. He locked it in the room with the body and they sent for a surgeon. The surgeon dissected the body and found the stomach walls were red and very vascular. There was a

'Oh my dear uncle! Oh my dear uncle!'

pint and a half of liquid in the stomach and he took this to be tested. Several different tests were performed in the presence of four or five other gentlemen and all the tests showed that there was evidence of arsenic in the liquid.

The pea soup wasn't tested. Instead it was given to a dog who immediately threw up. The dog did, however, survive. Constable Gardner was swiftly called for and Mary was taken away to be questioned.

At first Mary denied having ever purchased the arsenic. But, realising no doubt that Elizabeth Russell could prove that she had, she eventually admitted she had bought the poison to get rid of some rats. She said one lay dead under a chair in the house. The constable went to search the house and did find a dead mouse but, when it was cut open and examined, there was no evidence of it having swallowed arsenic. Mary also said she had no money but when she was searched a small box in her pocket contained five guineas and a purse contained one guinea, half-a-guinea and a seven shilling piece.

While taking her to the gaol Gardner asked, 'How could you be ever-persuaded to do such a thing?' Mary replied that she had not been persuaded by anyone and then confessed to having put two teaspoons of arsenic in a basin and pouring soup over it. As they were alone at the time Gardner asked her to repeat what she had said in front of witnesses when they arrived at the gaol.

At the inquest Mary said she had given Edward Clarke the two guineas and silver which the witnesses had seen him with. But later, when the inquest had concluded and Mary was being taken back to the gaol, the awful truth must have dawned on her and she realised the predicament she was in. She confessed more of the sorry tale to Gardner, telling him and another constable that it was Clarke who had instigated her into committing the murder – that it had all been his idea.

As a result, Edward Clarke was also arrested. Edward said he was present when William had eaten the soup and had seen him being sick later. Then early the next morning he had called at the house to find out how William was and was told that he had died. He insisted that he didn't know anything about the soup being poisoned.

At the Coventry Assizes on 3 August 1831 the counsel for Edward Clarke, Mr Pennington, asked Mr Justice Littledale if Clarke's trial could be removed from Coventry. He quoted the 'Act of the 38th of George the 3d, which vests a power in the court to remove the trial of a prisoner under circumstances such as are set forth in affidavits which I shall produce.'

The affidavits Mr Pennington put forward were from Edward and his solicitor which read that, due to the 'excited state of the public mind, the prisoner might not have a fair trial in Coventry.' Mr Justice Littledale reminded him that a case could only be removed to a neighbouring assizes, in this case Warwick. Mr Pennington agreed.

Mr Waddington, the counsel for Mary Higgins, asked the same question and then the prisoners themselves were asked if they were happy with standing trial at the Warwick Assizes. Both said they were. A fee of £40 each was charged and on payment their trials were adjourned until 9 August.

Here in Warwick they again appeared before Mr Justice Littledale, he being the judge who was travelling the Midland Circuit for the Summer Assizes. Mary and Edward's trials started at nine o'clock in the morning and continued for eleven hours. The reports wrote that they 'excited the most intense interest and the court was crowded to excess'.

The case against Edward Clarke lay on his being present when William had eaten the pea soup and the fact witnesses had queried that he seemed to have known that the old man was dead before it became common knowledge. He was also inconsistent with his statements as to his movements and those of William during the course of the evening. However, he made no secret of being at the house on the evening before William died and he maintained that he knew of the death through visiting the house on his way to work so his defence insisted that there was no case against him. No one could ever positively say that he knew the arsenic was in the soup or that he knew Mary had even bought any. Edward himself gave an address to the jury referring to the uncertainty of the evidence of his involvement and insisting his innocence. He also produced several character witnesses.

Mary on the other hand remained quiet throughout the trial and produced no character references. She pleaded her innocence but left her counsel to do the talking for her. Reporters giving the details of the case said she did have an air of modesty and innocence about her and, although the general opinion was that she was guilty, this countenance apparently produced feelings of compassion among those present in the court.

After deliberating for only six minutes the jury found Edward Clarke not guilty but Mary Ann Higgins guilty.

The judge then sentenced Mary to be executed at Coventry and her body to be taken for dissection. It was only now that Mary showed any emotion. As the judge passed sentence she began to cry and her cries could still be heard as she was led from the court. With this many others in the court, including some of the jury, shed a tear. During the trial Gardner had been severely reprimanded by the judge on the way he had questioned Mary when he first took her into custody and this, reports said, 'excited a strong indignation in the mind of every person in court'.

Mary was hanged two days later on Whitley Common. During the time she was awaiting her execution she talked very calmly about her death but often expressed her wish that Edward Clarke would suffer equally. She insisted that he had been involved and that it had been him who had put the idea into her head. It was even suggested that, when William had started being sick after eating the soup, Edward had said, 'Damn you, you have not given him enough.'

On the afternoon before her execution she was visited by her mother and her sister. She then read from the bible until eleven o'clock and asked the woman with her if she would read to her while she lay down. She fell asleep at one o'clock in the morning and slept until four. During the morning her mother came to see her again for the final time.

At midday on 11 August the crowds, who had gathered outside the gaol and along the streets leading to Whitley Common, saw Mary brought out of the gaol and put into the cart that would carry her to her execution. It must have been a sad sight to watch this young girl sitting on her own coffin as she was conveyed along Hay Lane.

Earl Street where Mary continued her journey. Very much altered today.

Hay Lane today where Mary started her journey to her execution; probably very unchanged.

Whitley Common. Now peaceful parkland on the outskirts of the city.

The journey took half an hour and passed along Earl Street, Much Park Street and London Road before arriving at Whitley Common. Here a crowd of 15,000 people had gathered to watch her execution. The accused stepped firmly from the cart and stood on the drop perfectly erect. After a prayer had been read the executioner removed her bonnet and replaced it with a large cap, which covered her face. He then adjusted the rope around her neck, tied her arms to her body and loosely tied a cord around her ankles. She stood unaided the whole of the time.

All was quiet for a couple of minutes then Mary dropped the white handkerchief signalling to the executioner she was ready. The bolt was pulled which opened the drop and Mary fell to her death.

After hanging for an hour her body was lowered into the coffin and taken to the Old Bridewell for dissection.

On 21 August 1831 the newspapers wrote:

On Friday se'night the County Surgeon and the four Parish Surgeons met at the Old Bridewell in this city for the purpose of dissecting the body of the unfortunate girl. After the first operation had been gone through the body was exhibited, as is customary on such occasions, to a great number of persons. It was particularly fat, and the internal parts presented a sound and healthy appearance.

The newspapers also published a letter which Mary had dictated to another prisoner while in gaol awaiting her trial:

I, Ann Higgins was born in Henley in Arden, I was brought up in the country with my grandfather twelve years ago: my schooling was at Miss Cattell's: at my grandfather's death I went to Manchester to my aunt and have been in service ever since: my parents gave me good advice but I did not listen to them: now I repent but it is too late: it causes my mother to shed many tears: but if she had the care of me it would not have happened, for the coming to Coventry to my uncle and having bad advice and bad company I am afraid will shorten my days but I hope it will be a warning to all youth to forsake bad company and obey their parents: I have been a sinner from my cradle but I hope the Lord will forgive me: bad company has brought me to this, for it has not been the neglect of my dear mother: I have a father in law [step-father] who is much better to me than my own father and all my friends: the first of my getting into bad company was with Edward Clarke three weeks before last Christmas day, but that bad company was not my own choosing, it was my uncles for he first brought him to see me that night and we kept company ever since.

To Edward Clarke she said, 'You are the first and only man I ever gave my hand; but may you never prosper, nor may you never thrive, nor anything you take in hand, so long as you have life. May the very ground you tread upon, grass refuse to grow. For you have been the only cause of this sorrow, grief and woe, Edward Clarke.'

Edward Clarke left Coventry with his father and brother, travelling from the city in a cart on the London Road. Here he had a good view of the gallows awaiting Mary. But he was recognised by furious passers-by and

The medieval houses of Spon Street which survived Hitler's bombs, 2013.

narrowly escaped with his life. No one could believe how callous he was. Later he was seen again with his father in Rugby, selling earthenware, but again he was recognised and forced to leave that town also. After this he disappeared ... or did he? An earthenware hawker named Edward Clarke, of the correct age, can be found on the 1861 and 1871 census living at Harnall Lane, Coventry, married with five children. Just a coincidence perhaps ... ?

Nearly 150 years later Mary was to turn up again. Her skull reappeared in 1972 having been thought at one time to have been kept, together with her bones, by a police surgeon and then at the School of Art and Design. It was bequeathed in a will and then donated to the Herbert Museum in Coventry.

CASE TWO   1844

MURDER IN LEICESTER ROW

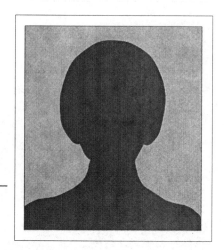

Suspect: Susannah Jarvis
Age: 13 or 14
Charge: Infanticide

The prisoner remained seated in the dock during the whole of her protracted trial on Tuesday, and maintained all the while a perfectly calm and indifferent demeanour, though her countenance is by no means one indicating dullness, or a lack of shrewd intelligence

Coventry Herald, 9 August 1844

Susannah Jarvis was born in Kenilworth in 1830. The baptism register there shows that she was baptised on 6 June 1830, the daughter of John, a comb-maker, and his wife Mary. In 1841 the family were living in New Row, Kenilworth.

That same year, Robert and Susan Goldsby were living in Leicester Row, Coventry, where Robert was a licensee of the Canal Tavern. The couple had two young children, Ann and Mary, and in following year, on 1 December 1842, they baptised another daughter at the Holy Trinity church and called her Emma.

Holy Trinity church on the corner of Priory Row and Cuckoo Lane, 2013.

In September 1843 the Goldsby's employed Susannah Jarvis as a nursemaid for Emma. However, it seems that for some reason the child didn't take to Susannah and, as the months went by, the dislike worsened. Finally, on 22 April 1844, Mrs Goldsby sent word to John and Mary Jarvis that she would be sending their daughter home two days later on the Wednesday.

Perhaps it was events of the previous Friday that had made Mrs Goldsby's mind up. On that evening she had bathed Emma then given her to Susannah to take for a walk. When they returned the child was put in her cradle to sleep but later Mrs Goldsby heard a sharp cry and, picking Emma up, she saw there were marks on the little girl's neck which had not been there when she had bathed the child. They resembled marks which could have been made by fingernails, pinching or scratching the skin. She asked Susannah if she knew how or when they could have appeared but Susannah said she knew nothing about them. No one else had been near the child or touched her while they had been out she said and she insisted she had not done anything herself.

However, on the following day little Emma seemed even more unwilling to go to Susannah and so another servant cared for her while Susannah was given other tasks to do. The weekend passed with no further incidents and on Monday Mrs Goldsby made arrangements to send Susannah home two days later. But later that day there was to be a tragic turn of events.

At around seven o'clock that evening, Mrs Goldsby left Emma asleep in her cradle in the back kitchen with Susannah while she washed her next youngest child, Mary, and took her up to bed. Her eldest daughter Ann was alone in the taproom eating some cake. On getting up the stairs Mrs Goldsby heard an anguished cry and called down asking what was wrong. When she didn't receive an answer she ran back downstairs and saw Susannah moving away from the cradle wiping her hands on her pinafore. On seeing Mrs Goldsby, Susannah cried out that a man had killed, or stabbed, the baby and had run down the yard. When questioned, Mrs Goldsby could never remember whether Susannah had used the word 'stabbed' or 'killed'. Mrs Goldsby knew, however, that she had only left Emma for four minutes so she could not comprehend how this could have happened in so short a time. She picked her baby up, saying, 'No it's no man – it's you I doubt', and ran out through the front door screaming murder! Emma's hair was covered in blood and several people came to help Mrs Goldsby but on taking the child from her could see it was dead.

Someone sent for a surgeon, and neighbour John Griffin went into the house to look for evidence. He found a knife, still wet with blood, lying on the dresser in the back kitchen, near to where the cradle stood.

'ran out through the front door screaming murder!'

When John Overton, the surgeon, arrived Griffin handed it to him, who in turn handed it to the police constable who had been called.

Police Constable Salmon examined the cradle and stated that he 'found a great deal of blood on the clothes and the pillow. On the wall, close to which the cradle stood, were spirtles of blood and on the dresser were two streaks of blood, as if they had run from the knife.'

Susannah Jarvis came into the room while he was there saying, 'I'm sure it was not me that did it; look at my hands how clean they are.' Police Inspector John Vice, who arrived soon after, wasn't so sure and had a few questions for her to answer. Susannah said she had gone out into the yard to use the privy and it was then that she heard the baby scream. Going back in she had seen a tall man without shoes and stockings. When asked if she would recognise him again she said she wouldn't. Her clothes were inspected it was found that the bodice of her dress had spots of blood on it and her pinafore was crumpled in the middle as if she had used it to wipe her hands. It also bore a reddish stain around this area. There were also several spots of blood at the bottom of her pinafore. She said the spots of blood on her bodice were caused by her having leant across the dresser and those on her pinafore were from falling down in the yard. But there was no evidence of blood in the yard.

Rumours were also circulating that the child had been killed by its older sister who was playing the game of 'sticking pigs' which imitated the killing of pigs. This rumour was dispelled at the inquest.

Leicester Row today.

The inquest was held at the Wheel Tavern in Leicester Row on the evenings of 23 and 24 April and newspapers described Susannah as being 'a thin, and rather agreeable, sharp-looking country girl'. On her first appearance she appeared indifferent to her situation, almost pert, and not the sort of girl who would have committed such a crime. She showed no sympathy or feelings of emotion, which would have suggested she was innocent, but at the same time there was no betrayal in her voice or any agitation which would show her guilt. On the second day, however, she was very different, with reports stating that she seemed faint and disheartened. Her mother was with her and Police Inspector Vice was commended on his conduct towards her. It seemed he took into account her age and sex, and his manner was very gentle towards her. He made sure she was comfortable and if she felt hungry he saw that she had something to eat.

At her first appearance at the inquest Susannah's father had been in the room to put questions to the witnesses but Mr Lea, who was acting as the prosecution, advised him to ask his questions through the coroner or to engage a lawyer to act for Susannah. The following evening a solicitor, Mr Morris, appeared on behalf of Susannah.

At the start of the inquest the surgeon described the injury:

> The knife had penetrated just above the sternum or chest bone; and being driven in an oblique direction, it severed the jugular vein, separated the carotid artery, wounding a portion of the lungs and entering the chest; it terminated its course at the posterior part of the body, between the fourth and fifth ribs, almost perforating the skin and the outside, making the depth of it betwixt five and six inches.

Ann Goldsby said that after her mother had taken her sister Mary upstairs she had gone out of the front door to see if any of her playmates were about. At the same time she saw Susannah in the backyard who told her she was going to the privy, Ann didn't see, however, whether she did or not and whether she just turned back into the house. On going back inside Ann heard her baby sister crying.

Neighbours came forward saying they had seen a strange man in the area. One, 'a woman named Watts', said she was walking from Tower Street to Leicester Street that Monday evening and remembered seeing a 'travelling man or beggar' with no shoes and stockings coming from the Cottage public house. He was a short distance behind her and then he was gone. She didn't know where. She supposed that the nearest she saw him to the Canal Tavern was about 100 yards away. 'He was not a very tall man, and rather stooped in the shoulders.'

The canal bank where Thomas King saw a man sitting, 2013.

Thomas King said he had seen a man with no shoes on sitting on a bank around the corner from Leicester Street. He had his head down, as if looking at something in his hands.

Despite these seemingly exonerating statements the coroner's jury decided that Susannah Jarvis was guilty of 'wilful murder' and she was sent for trial at the next assizes.

The newspapers reported that:

The prisoner received the announcement of the verdict with comparative calmness; told her mother never to mind, and not to cry, for that she (meaning herself) had done nothing. Altogether the concluding scene was painful and impressive. The counsel of her parents, on parting with her, desiring her not to eat or drink anything, whoever might offer her food, and to resist all entreaties to do so, but to pine herself to death in prison, was an exhibition of moral deformity and perversity of spirit on their part, indicating bias in the parental influence with the child.

The police were already undertaking their inquiries at local lodging houses, trying to find the man Susannah had described but to no avail. Eventually the tollgate keeper, Townsend, said he thought he knew who it was. Others agreed – yes it was the 'miserable fiddler, named Jones or Davis, who lives at Foleshill.' But no one had seen him in Leicester Row that night.

The Coventry Assizes took place in August and Susannah made her appearance on Tuesday the 6th before Mr Justice Coltman at nine o'clock in the morning. The jury consisted of men from many parts of Warwickshire and of various occupations – a steel toymaker from Edgbaston, farmers from Over Whitacre, Stoke and Corley, a silk dealer from Stoke and an agent from Edgbaston – all sat listening to the evidence for eight and a half hours. The council for the prosecution, Mr Mellor, brought in witnesses who had been in the area that night who said they had not seen a man come from the alleyway, while Susannah's defence lawyer, Mr Humphrey, brought people in who had seen this man. It was noted, however, that none of these had actually seen him coming from the back of the tavern. Mr Humphrey asked the jury to consider what motive they thought Susannah had. But, in his address to

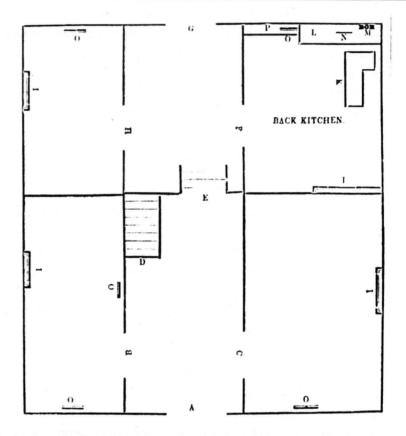

Newspaper cutting showing its readers a plan of the house. (*Coventry Herald*, 26 April 1844)

A The front door leading from Leicester-row into the Canal Tavern.
B The door leading into the bar.
C Door of the front kitchen.
D The stairs.
E The steps down into the passage, leading to the back-kitchen, back parlour and
 back door.
F Door of the back-kitchen where the murder took place.
G The back-door from the passage into the yard, out of which there is a road bearing
 to the right hand, into Leicester-street.
H The back parlour door.
I Fire places of the different rooms.
K The cradle in the back-kitchen where the infant lay.
L The dresser.
M The knife-box on the dresser.
N The position of the carving-knife when found, lying upon the dresser wet with blood.
O Windows of the different rooms.
P Washing sink and kitchen apparatus.

the jury, Mr Mellor asked equally what motive a poor beggar would have for murdering a baby.

Susannah was given good character references. The Revd Mr Parry, vicar of Kenilworth, said she was a kind-hearted girl. Mrs Swaine, mistress of the National School at Kenilworth, described her in a similar way. But again Mr Mellor asked why had Susannah not cried out murder when she had seen what had happened.

The trial finished at half past five and the jury consulted for a quarter of an hour but then asked if they could retire. At half past seven they asked if they could have some water. They then spent the night locked in the court house and at half past six the next morning were given a supply of bread and milk. At ten o'clock the court reopened but the jury still hadn't come to a decision so the judge ordered that the prisoner be remanded till the next assizes. On 27 March 1845 Susannah appeared before Mr Justice Maule and a new set of jurors. Her defence brought forward a new suggestion that the spots of blood on the wall, being high up, could only have been made by someone taller. The jury now only took twenty minutes to find Susannah not guilty.

In 1851 she is back living with her parents in Kenilworth. The previous year to this she had given birth to a daughter, Betsy, who was baptised in Kenilworth on 13 October 1850. Susannah married George Barber in Kenilworth on 13 August 1854 and they went on to have five children. She lived in Kenilworth all her life, dying at the age of 85 in 1916 and taking with her the secret of what did actually happen that night.

CASE THREE 1844

ALL FOR A SOVEREIGN

Suspect: George Skelsey
Age: About 30
Charge: Manslaughter

Whitehall. May 9, 1844. Gentlemen – I am directed by the secretary Sir James Graham to acknowledge the receipt of your application dated the 7th instant, and in reply, to acquaint you that a reward of £100 will be paid by Government for the apprehension of a man named George Skelsey, against whom a verdict of guilty for the murder of Henry Cluley has been found by the Jury of the Coroner's inquest. I have the honour to be, gentlemen, your obedient servant, S.N. Phillips.

Coventry Herald, 17 May 1844

Just five days after the murder of baby Emma Goldsby another murder took place in the Coventry area. Henry Cluley was a 50-year-old silk weaver who lived at Sowe Waste, a couple of miles out of Coventry in the Walsgrave on Sowe parish. He lived with his younger sister Elizabeth and their niece Elizabeth Farn, the daughter of another sister, Margaret.

William Eaves was an old man who had known Henry Cluley for twenty-three years. One Saturday evening, 27 April 1844, he overtook Henry while walking out of Courthouse Green in the Foleshill parish of Coventry. It was about eight o'clock. They walked together as far as the Eburn's bridge and here they parted company: Cluley to cross the fields to his home in Church Close and Eaves to cross the bridge to meet a friend before going into the Boat Inn.

As he walked up the bridge, Eaves saw George Skelsey also crossing and, as they passed one another, he heard Skelsey shout to someone in a boat, 'Have not you heard me talk to you about the b____r that owes me a sovereign.' An answer came back, 'Yes I have George.' Eaves wasn't clear whether George Skelsey was answering his friend in the boat or just muttering to himself, but he then heard Skelsey say, 'Now I'll go and pay the b____r' as he made to go after Henry Cluley. Skelsey ran across the bridge and into the fields and William Eaves saw him knock Cluley to the ground.

Henry called to William for help, 'Bill you won't see me murdered will you?' and William rushed to his aid. But Skelsey was shouting, 'Say one word, I'll serve you the same and throw you into the canal and drown you.'

Meanwhile, David Budd and Francis Deeming were also walking along the towpath. Deeming had heard Skelsey say to Cluley, 'Do you mean to give me the sovereign you owe me?' and when he saw Skelsey attack Henry he shouted, 'For God's sake George don't kill the man.' Skelsey had answered, 'You old b____r if you say anything to me, I'll serve you the same; or anyone else that takes his part.'

Canal and towpath leading from Courthouse Green to what was known as Sowe Waste, 2013.

By now William Eaves had joined the group and was helping Cluley to his feet. He then tried to calm Skelsey down as he led him back down the towpath to the bridge. After picking up the reticule, stick and can he had dropped, Cluley followed slowly behind. Eaves talked to Skelsey as they walked in an effort to defuse the situation, but, as they were nearing the bridge, Skelsey turned and knocked Cluley down again. Deeming and Budd pulled Skelsey away as Cluley got to his feet. They then kept talking to Skelsey as Cluley staggered off, heading for home this time; not bothering to pick his things up. But no sooner had they let him go than Skelsey ran in the same direction shouting that he would give him another 'putting-up'. As he climbed over the stile they noticed that Skelsey was wearing heavy, strong nailed boots.

The remaining men decided they should call at Henry Cluley's house to make sure he was all right. However, when they got there they discovered Skelsey had beat them to it and was shouting at Cluley's sister, 'I've done your b____r of a brother and I'll do the same for you before I sleep.' They saw

'I've done your b____r of a brother'

Cluley lying on his back on the floor but thought he had only fainted and shouted to his sister to get some water to bathe his face. But Henry Cluley was dead and George Skelsey had run off.

Henry's niece, Elizabeth Farn, said Skelsey had arrived at the house shortly before her uncle. She had heard Skelsey threatening her aunt and had gone to see what was going on. Henry had then staggered to the door and she had helped him in but, before she could sit him on a chair, he had sighed and slumped to the floor.

When a surgeon, Mr Charles Henry Parson, examined the body he found a fracture in front of the windpipe an inch in length and one on the right side which actually went through the windpipe. He said this one would have caused suffocation and death and could not have been done by a fist, only by a kick from a boot.

Had Skelsey attacked Cluley again when nobody was about or was the fatal wound inflicted during one of those two attacks witnessed by Eaves, Deeming and Budd? The answer was not known but the jury at the coroner's inquest were of a common view that Cluley had died through injuries which Skelsey had inflicted and they found a verdict of wilful murder against George Skelsey. The coroner issued a warrant for his apprehension and a reward notice was published in the newspaper.

Skelsey was eventually arrested by James Isaacs, the superintendent of the rural police for Warwickshire, on 18 May in Wakefield, Yorkshire.

It seems someone had seen there was a reward and come forward, because on that same day Isaacs made his way to Manchester. He made inquiries and then, on the information he received there, Isaacs set out for Huddersfield in Yorkshire. Discovering that Skelsey and his brother-in-law had bought train tickets, Isaacs made his way to Wakefield station where he found them standing by a door in the station. As he approached them, Skelsey's brother-in-law said, 'I put this man in your charge.' Was he, then, the mystery informer?

Isaacs handcuffed Skelsey, and together they travelled back to Warwickshire. They went by train to Derby and then on to Rugby where Skelsey was left in the custody of the local police.

After the attacks Skelsey had gone to his aunt's public house, the Spotted Dog. John Sidwell was in the pub at the time and said that George Skelsey was swearing and shouting. His aunt, Mrs Hayes, asked him what the matter was, adding, 'Have you been down to Harry's?' He said he had been and 'had titivated him up nicely'. He threw out his right leg and said, 'D__n my eyes aunt if my hind foot isn't as good as a fore foot to me.' He then held his arms up and threw himself back, making a noise like someone having a fit or dying. His aunt said, 'George if you have done anything to Harry you had better be off for the police will be here directly.'

'I don't care a d__n for any policeman in England for no one man shall take me.' He added that one country was as good as another to him, so he was going to Halifax in Yorkshire and then leaving the country. No one would find him.

George Skelsey's first appearance in front of the public was at the petty sessions in the parish of Ansty on the outskirts of Coventry and newspapers wrote that 'a great concourse of persons attended to obtain a sight of the wretched man'. He arrived with Isaacs at a quarter to eleven and the newspapers described him as a good-looking man, aged about 30, of 5ft 6in but quite stout. He was decently and respectably dressed as a boatman. Over his clothes he wore a brown-coloured smock frock.

He was immediately taken into the justice's room and was given an armchair while other business of the day was completed. During a break he was served bread and cheese and a small glass of ale. There were a lot of people looking through the windows from outside. Some he knew and he occasionally nodded at them.

Eventually he was brought before the Bench and the witnesses told their stories. He contradicted Elizabeth Farn's statement and said that her aunt 'had taken pretty good care to teach her niece a pretty good tale'. He criticised the fact that the aunt hadn't been called to give evidence and no reason was given for her not appearing. He added that Cluley was as bad as himself.

Skelsey was found guilty of wilful murder and sent for trial at the next assizes. Up until this point he had shown no signs of distress but now he wept bitterly.

He later appeared at the Summer Assizes in Coventry before Lord Chief Justice Denman. The whole day had been spent on the Susannah Jarvis trial and, when the jury had retired on that case, a new one was sworn in. Skelsey's defence lawyer, Mr Humfrey, argued that the case was not one of wilful murder and must be treated as manslaughter. After some debate the jury seemed to have agreed with this view and, when they did find him guilty, it was of manslaughter. George Skelsey therefore escaped the death sentence and Lord Chief Justice Denman sentenced him to ten years transportation. He set sail on the *Sir Robert Peel* on 6 September 1844 and arrived in Van Dieman's Land (Tasmania) on 6 May 1845.

On 22 October at Ansty Petty Sessions it was decided that the £100 reward would be shared among three people: James Isaacs got £40 and two boatmen, W. Richardson, £40 and John Tuckey, £20.

On 25 September 1854 Henry Cluley's sister Elizabeth married William Eaves at Walsgrave parish church. It would appear from the register he was the widowed son of the man who had tried to help her brother.

CASE FOUR   1845

MURDER IN BERKESWELL

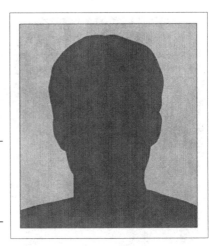

Suspect: James Read
Age: 19 or 20
Charge: Murder

Here the horrid scene presented itself of the body of the old man lying dead, from a desperate blow on the back of the head. His skull being literally shattered by the brutal onslaught which had been made upon him. At a short distance lay the axe with which the murder had been perpetrated, and bearing sickening marks of the foul purpose it had been used for, smeared as it was by the blood and grey hairs of the murdered man

Coventry Herald, 21 November 1845

Thomas Tranter lived in a secluded spot, running his small farm and leading a solitary life in his comfortable cottage in the village of Berkeswell in the countryside surrounding Coventry. His only companion was George Satchwell, a young boy of only 10 years of age, who came each day from his home in Burton Green, 2 miles away, to work on the farm. George had known Tranter for three or four years but had only been working for him about one week. He brought his own victuals from home but would go into the house at mealtimes to have them.

On Monday, 17 November 1845 Satchwell had his breakfast with Thomas and then went off to work. He fetched a shovel and fork from the barn and went into the meadow to spread manure. After ten minutes Tranter went out to him to tell him to spread the manure more thinly. He spent a short time showing George how this should be done then went round to the back of the house and George didn't see him again.

A row of cottages in Berkeswell, 2013.

It was only a quarter of an hour later that George looked up at the house and saw that the shutters were closed. About half an hour or three quarters of an hour later he saw a young man come out of the front door, shut it, then lock it and put the key in his pocket. George didn't know who the man was but he could see he was wearing a dark waistcoat, with light sleeves and back, had a black hat on and was carrying a bundle under his arm tied with a blue handkerchief.

At lunchtime George made his way over to the house but couldn't get in. It was all very quiet with the door still locked and the shutters closed. His dinner was locked inside the house so he went to the pump for some water. Although he was no doubt disappointed at the prospect of having no dinner, he didn't find it unusual as Thomas often locked up and went off for business purposes occasionally.

George tried the door three times during the course of the day and then when it started to get dark he went home.

On the next day the cottage was still locked and bolted, but again no concern was shown. It wasn't until the Wednesday that George started asking if anyone had seen Thomas Tranter. He went to John Whitehead, the blacksmith, who informed Thomas Trippas, the constable of Berkswell. Together Whitehead and Trippas went back to Tranter's cottage.

Constable Trippas found a ladder against a window upstairs and climbing up he broke open the window and got into the room, followed by John Whitehead.

The newspapers described the scene the two men had discovered:

They examined the room and found the chests opened, and their drawers partly out, their contents in confusion, and a quantity of writings and paper about the rooms and on the bed. On going down stairs they found a candlestick, with part of a candle in it, as if it had been blown out, standing between the doors: there were eight or ten bags and some string lying in the kitchen, a flat-sided bottle, with some sort of liquor, on the table; saw a saucer with butter in it, sugar basin with sugar in it, and a quantity of apparel, some as if pulled off while wet. On finding nothing Police Constable Samuel Holmes of Coventry was sent for and he made a thorough search of the house.

It was going into the outhouse that they made their grisly find.

A body lay on the ground covered in a sack and a large quantity of blood, which had run from that body and formed a dry, coagulated puddle. When Holmes lifted the sack they found what they now fully expected to find. Thomas Tranter lay on his right side, his face on the ground. He had just one severe wound at the back of the head, at least 3in long, and it was from this that the large quantity of blood had run. The brains could quite clearly be seen through the gaping wound. An axe and a bill-hook lay close by to

'The brains could quite clearly be seen through the gaping wound'

the body. Both were covered with blood so it seems that both had been used on Thomas Tranter, ensuring that he was dead. The axe also had grey hairs stuck to the congealed blood.

At the inquest held at the Black Bear Inn in Berkswell, William Iliffe, a neighbouring farmer, stated that he had seen a young local man

The Black Bear Inn, Berkeswell, 2013.

called James Read coming from the direction of Tranter's house on the Monday morning. He was wearing a dark waistcoat with light sleeves and back. John Wright, who lived in Docker's Lane, also saw James Read – wearing a dark cloth-fronted waistcoat with light sleeves and brown narrow-cord trousers. He had recognised the clothes as Read had worn them all summer while working for Thomas Rotherham. But the thing John Wright noticed as being different from James Read's normal attire, was that he was wearing a black fur hat, when he always wore a Scotch cap. Tranter's nephew, John Whitehead, said his uncle had a black beaver hat. Read was also seen by a third person, Henry Stephenson. He was certain it was Read. He said he couldn't be mistaken as he had known him for about five years.

George Hopkins from Balsall also knew James Read and he had seen him on the Wednesday on a footpath, 5.5 miles from Birmingham. Read had told him he was just on his way home from Birmingham after looking for employment there but hadn't found anything.

The inquest also heard from Police Constable Holmes that, when searching outside Tranter's cottage, footprints had been found in the freshly dug ground. They were shown to a shoemaker, Joseph Blick of Balsall, who had said, 'The first footmark I saw struck me as being similar to a boot I made for James Read; it was a straight boot, a short size for a man, there were two rows of square-headed nails.'

James Read had been lodging with Thomas and Ann Hyatt from the beginning of July until 22 November. But he had since disappeared. A reward for £100 for the capture of James Read appeared in the *Police Gazette*:

> Is described as about 19 or 20 years of age, 5 foot 4 inches high, stout made, and when talking has a smiling countenance; had on a pair of narrow cord trousers, which had a hole in the left thigh, and is supposed to have with him an old pair of plaid trousers and an old dark jacket, which he may be wearing. He is believed to be in the neighbourhood of Birmingham.

On Sunday, 7 December Police Constable Holmes received a letter from the police in Aylesbury saying they had apprehended a man who answered to the description in every detail of that of James Read. Holmes immediately went off to Aylesbury but, when he saw the man in the gaol, he had his doubts as to whether this could really be the accused. He was certainly the same height as Read and had the same colour hair and eyes. His cord trousers even had a hole in the left knee and bloodstains on them. The man was taken back to Coventry and here witnesses confirmed what Holmes thought. Those who knew James Read well said it wasn't him. Although they did say that the likeness was so good they did hesitate at first. The man was discharged and his fare back to Aylesbury paid for.

It wasn't until two months later in February 1846 that the real James Read was apprehended.

Following the murder he had gone to Bilston in Staffordshire and found work as a miner using the name James Jones. Then he moved to Birmingham and it was on that first day back in Birmingham that he was recognised in the street.

Read had once worked for a Mr Page, a milkman, and he happened to be walking along Dale End when he saw Read. Page stopped him and asked how he was and where he was working. The two chatted and Read explained that he had been working in the coal-pits in Bilston and had only just arrived in Birmingham a few hours before. It was while they were talking that Page's servant, Sampson Barnett, came up and recognised Read. 'Here's the man there's a hundred pound's reward for,' Barnett told Page. But Read answered, 'If I'd been the man wouldn't I have been taken long ago?' and walked away.

Page and his servant followed Read at a safe distance, hoping to see a policeman. When they didn't they caught up with him and asked him to go to the police station with them. He refused so they grabbed him by the collar and while he was struggling a policeman did arrive. He was taken to the lock-up still protesting his innocence and from there taken back to Coventry to appear before the magistrates. He was charged with murder and escorted to the gaol by Police Constable Samuel Holmes to await his trial at the next Warwick Assizes, which took place at the end of March 1846.

Here Mr Miller, his defence lawyer, gave a powerful and impressive address arguing the fact that there was no real proof that Read had committed the murder. It was mere coincidence that he had been seen in the area at the time. On the strength of this the jury found James Read not guilty.

However, within two weeks Read had been rearrested. This time on a charge of robbing the home of Thomas Tranter. The police were determined to get their man. Articles which were said to have belonged to Tranter – one hat, one handkerchief and one shirt – were found to have been pawned by

Newspaper cutting advertising the sale of Thomas Tranter's property. *Coventry Herald*, 31 July 1846.

James Read. Tranter's sister swore to having made the shirt for him twenty years previously. And the woman who did his washing recognised the hand-kerchief. She said she had washed it two months before his death and had seen him wearing it around his neck afterwards. He was said to have had two hats, but one had disappeared and only one had been found after the murder.

James Read now appeared before the assizes in August 1846 and this time, after consulting for a quarter of an hour, the jury found him guilty of robbery. Mr Justice Colbridge then made a statement:

James Read, the Jury, after a long consultation, had found themselves compelled to come to the conclusion that you are guilty of the charge which had been laid against you. That charge is only one of larceny, in having stolen some property which lately belonged to a farmer of the name of Tranter, who it unfortunately appeared had met with his end by the violent and wicked act of some person or persons unknown. You yourself have been previously indicted as having been concerned in this diabolical transaction and the result of that was that you were acquitted. Those who were in the habit of attending Courts of Justice well knew that charges of so grave and serious a description of those as murder were very diligently considered; and unless the evidence adduced in support of those charges was brought clearly and convincingly home to the minds of the Jury, that body were in the habit of returning a verdict of Not Guilty. I say not now whether or not you were really guilty of the murder of Tranter or not; that is now entirely a matter between yourself and your Creator; but still you have to answer to a larceny which was evidently committed under circumstances of a very aggravated nature, because I cannot believe that you were the person who rifled the boxes on Tranter's premises, and the same who left the house under such painful circumstances, that I forbear further to allude to, in order to dispose of the articles mentioned, in the manner you did. Such a case of larceny was not an ordinary one; and coupled with other circumstances, I feel it my duty to pass upon you a somewhat severe sentence. It is no real severity to you to send you out of the country you are now in; and if you yourself possess any feeling at all, you cannot but consider it best. The sentence of the court, therefore, is that you be transported beyond the seas, to such place as her Majesty in Council shall think fit, for the term of seven years.

During the trial James Read never said a word but as the judge passed sentence tears began to trickle down his cheeks. He was still crying as he left the dock.

On 28 February 1851 a convict ship called *The Cornwall* set sail from England bound for Van Dieman's Land, filled with convicts, one of which was James Read.

CASE FIVE 1859

ALL THROUGH HER FATHER

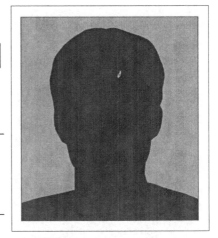

Suspect:	John Kington
Age:	22
Charge:	Murder

On Saturday morning a murder of a very deliberate and atrocious character was committed in Coventry, and as a similar occurrence has not taken place in that city for a considerable time, it has necessarily occasioned the greatest excitement. The perpetrator of the fearful deed is a young man, 22 years of age, named John Kington, by trade a ribbon weaver, but who has for some time enjoyed the appellation of a 'knob-stick', a designation applied to such artisans as work for manufacturers under price.

Birmingham Daily Post, 14 November 1859

On 5 April 1858 it seems, according to the parish registers of St Michael's, numerous marriages took place. Perhaps this was because it was Easter Monday. Hopefully the others were happy marriages, but it was only a year later that one of these marriages was to end in tragedy.

John Kington and Elizabeth Holmes were one of the couples to get married that day and later that month their daughter Martha Elizabeth was born on 29 April. Perhaps due to the circumstances which followed she wasn't baptised until 4 January 1860.

John was a drummer in the Warwickshire Militia and his comrades often commented on him having a violent temper. In 1851 he is living in White Friars Lane, Coventry, with his parents and other siblings and working as a ribbon weaver. That same year Elizabeth was living at Primrose Terrace off East Street with her father, Samuel Holmes, and her

St Michael's, Coventry Cathedral, before the bombs were dropped.

mother and siblings. Samuel was also employed as a weaver but, ten years earlier, on the 1841 census, Samuel had been a police officer. In fact he was the police constable involved in the investigation of the previous case, Thomas Tranter. Why Samuel retired from the police at the age of 35 and became a weaver is not known but he was certainly still in the police force in Coventry until at least May 1849, as he made appearances at the police court up until then. There was a rumour that he was dismissed through drunkenness. Whatever the reason, it was Samuel who was to be, however unintentionally, the cause of the tragedy.

The quarrels began a year after John and Elizabeth had married and, between June and August 1859, Elizabeth went back to live with her parents. John persuaded Elizabeth to return and they found a room together. But soon the quarrels began again and, after being accused of ill-treatment, Kington was ordered to keep the peace for three months.

It was her father Samuel Holmes who had persuaded Elizabeth to go to the magistrates to have John bound over. She hadn't wanted to and had refused to go but her father had sent for a constable to take her there. At first John was unable to find the sureties and ended up in prison which only increased his bitterness towards Samuel Holmes. But when the sureties had been found John was released and constantly followed his wife around, asking her to go back to him. She refused, usually on the grounds that her father was against it. The three months had been due to expire on 22 November.

Eleven days before, on 11 November, a Friday evening, John and Elizabeth were standing talking in East Street when her two brothers came up. They called to her, 'Come out of that, don't be talking to such a villain as that.' It seems she ignored them so her brothers went straight home and told their father. He went immediately to East Street and finding her still there with John took her home.

After that John said he then spent a miserable and restless night, and made his mind up to meet his wife in the morning on her way to work. Intent on what he was going to do he took a large table knife with him. Elizabeth worked at Green's factory in East Street and John actually met up with her during her breakfast break at eight o'clock. They walked along East Street, into Paynes Lane and out towards the fields around Coventry. Elizabeth then said she would have to get back to work as her half-hour break was almost over.

East Street today.

'You shall not go back to your work this morning; you had better come home with me,' John told her. Again she said her father would not allow it. 'If I do, my father says he will murder me,' she said. With that John took the knife out and stabbed and slashed her repeatedly in her neck.

John's description of her last moments were, 'She faintly and with difficulty articulated, with blood gurgling in her half-severed throat – it's all through my father. God bless you Jack. Goodbye. It's all through my father.'

'blood gurgling in her half-severed throat'

That was the story of what had happened that morning according John Kington. Other witnesses described the scene somewhat differently.

A milkman, Henry Quiney, had passed them in East Street and heard part of the conversation. John was asking how she and the baby were and Quiney heard Elizabeth tell John it was nothing to do with him; 'You only want to take me down the lane because there is no one about, you rogue.'

Paynes Lane today.

Mary Ann Pickard was walking from Geoffrey Wood's Cross to Paynes Lane when she heard a woman scream. She looked over the hedge and saw a man and woman struggling. He placed his knee on the woman's breast and threw her down. Mary saw the man had a knife and that the woman put her hands up twice and heard her ask him to forgive her. A reply came, 'No, I've forgiven you times enough, if your father had been here I would have served him the same.' Whilst this was said Mary could see that he was cutting the woman's throat but was too horrified to do anything.

James Jones, a street contractor, and James Edwards, a labourer, also saw the struggle and rushed over to the spot. But they were so horrified seeing John plunging the knife at Elizabeth that at first they were also paralysed to the spot. Jones was the first to recover and rushed to fetch a policeman.

Kington then threw the knife down and asked Edwards to go to the police station with him where he was going to give himself up. In the event they met Police Constable Salmon on his way to the field.

'Mr Salmon I am here. I will go with you quietly; so don't handle me,' John said. Salmon asked where the knife was and John made no attempt to cover up what had happened. 'It lays bedside her. She's dead enough.

It was her father's fault, and if she had come and lived with me last night it would not have happened, but I am satisfied now. She should ha' been ruled by me and not by her father.'

Later in his cell he also said, 'I am glad my wife is out of the way so that she cannot be pulled and mauled about by her father and I can die happy now it is done. I did it with my left arm; my right arm trembled so and fell to my side useless.'

Kington always insinuated that there was an incestuous relationship between Elizabeth and her father but Samuel strenuously denied this. He wrote to the newspapers telling of the 'gross imputations being made upon his character' and that 'vague, yet serious charges, had been circulated to his prejudice'. He said it was also untrue that he had been dismissed from the police force for drunkenness.

The newspapers reported Kington's appearance at the police court and the interest the public had in him:

> Long before the time appointed a great crowd had assembled near the County Hall and no sooner were the doors open than the building was quickly and densely filled in every part, and so anxious were persons to get a sight of the murderer that they lingered round the doors, and as those who were tired of the pressure within left the building, there was a rush to get possession of the place vacated. The prisoner, on entering the dock, appeared nothing moved but perfectly self-possessed.

Kington was charged and ordered to appear at the next assizes in Warwick in December.

On 7 December a newspaper wrote: 'As the day of the trial approaches the unhappy man, Kington, appears at times much more thoughtful. The Chaplain of the Gaol pays him much attention; also within the last few days some of his nearest relatives have had an interview with him and he appears anxious about his fate.'

The trial took place on 20 December and as John had never made any secret of his involvement in the murder or the intention to commit it, either to the police or the magistrates, it was no surprise that when asked how he pleaded he answered 'guilty.' The judge asked if he had anything to say why sentence of death should not be passed upon him. He didn't answer.

With that Mr Justice Williams put on the black cap and said:

> The sentence of the Court upon you is, that you be taken hence to the place whence you came and thence to the place of execution; that you be hanged by your neck till you are dead, and then that you shall be buried within the precincts of the Gaol where you have been confined; and may God have mercy on your soul.

During the judge's speech, Kington had sighed heavily and then begun to sob bitterly. As soon as the judge had finished his statement Kington turned and hurried from the dock. He only reached as far down as the second step, however, before he fainted into the arms of the gaoler. In ten days' time he would be facing the executioner.

On the Thursday afternoon, 29 December, John was visited by his mother, father and brother and sisters for them to make their final goodbyes. His daughter was also taken to see him and once again impudent suggestions were made, questioning the child's real father, with the newspapers referring to her as 'the innocent cause of the dreadful deed'. Was there some rumours that Samuel was the father of his own daughter's child?

The following morning John Kington was taken out to the scaffold and here he asked if he could say a few words to the crowd. He began, 'My dear friends, I hope this will be a warning to you ...' But the crowds shouted and made such a noise that they couldn't hear him and he stopped speaking. Perhaps he wanted to say that he had forgiven his father-in-law, we'll never know.

The executioner fixed the noose and put the cap over Kington's head. After a minute, during which time Kington appeared to be fervently praying, he dropped the handkerchief and the bolt was drawn. 'He struggled considerably for two minutes and a half, when all muscular action ceased.'

His was the first execution in Warwick for twelve years and led newspapers to comment that public opinion of hangings had changed and now 'a public execution of a notorious criminal, excites only sorrow and sadness, and that the morbid curiosity which originated a "chamber of horrors" has nearly passed away not only from the educated but also from the lowest classes of society.' In fact, on the Friday morning of the execution, it was said that there were only a few stragglers seen wending their way to Warwick along the Birmingham and Coventry roads. In the end 700 to 800 people witnessed the execution and a few hundred were disappointed. There had been secrecy as to the exact time of the hanging and they turned up too late, thinking the execution was at eleven o'clock.

How true John's accusations were regarding his father-in-law will never be known. But Samuel Holmes was determined to clear his name and wrote the following letter to the Coventry magistrates:

Worshipful Sir, – I trust you will pardon my presumption in writing to you in reference to the late melancholy occurrence, the murder of my daughter, as in connection therewith the most shameful and unfounded charges have been circulated, very injurious to my character.

One of the newspaper reports of the incidents of the murder is full of falsehoods, to pander to the morbid tastes of the public. These false reports are so horrid a nature that I earnestly hope you will request your Brother Visiting Justices, with yourself, to give me and my witnesses an opportunity of coming before you, that you may hear them in refutation of the vile and groundless charges made against me. I feel it is due to myself and the character of my other children in after life, that the whole affair should be investigated, when I have no fear of appearing before you at the close of the enquiry exonerated and innocent of these base imputations. If you, gentlemen, will kindly grant me this, and direct Mr Mann, the Governor of the Gaol, to give me notice when you will assemble, I shall be extremely obliged, in order that the public mind may be disabused and set right upon this very painful affair.

The Justice of the Peace, T.S. Morris, replied that he was unable to 'interfere in the matter in question', that all the relevant documents were in the hands of the police.

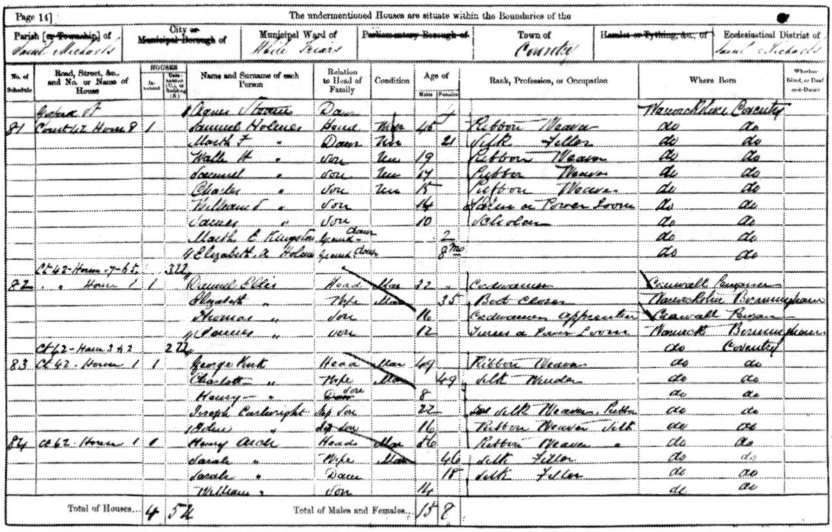

Page 14] The undermentioned Houses are situate within the Boundaries of the

Parish ~~[or Township]~~ of	City ~~or Municipal Borough~~ of	Municipal Ward of	~~Parliamentary Borough of~~	Town of	~~Hamlet or Tything, &c., of~~	Ecclesiastical District of
Saint Michaels		White Friars		Coventry		Saint Michaels

No. of Schedule	Road, Street, &c., and No. or Name of House	Houses Inhabited	Houses Uninhabited (U.), or Building (B.)	Name and Surname of each Person	Relation to Head of Family	Condition	Age of Males	Age of Females	Rank, Profession, or Occupation	Where Born	Whether Blind, or Deaf-and-Dumb
	Gosford St			Agnes Stratton	Daur					Warwickshire Coventry	
81	Court No 2 House 8	1		Samuel Holmes	Head	Widr	46		Ribbon Weaver	do do	
				Martha F "	Daur	Unm		21	Silk Filler	do do	
				Walter H "	Son	Unm	19		Ribbon Weaver	do do	
				Samuel "	Son	Unm	17		Ribbon Weaver	do do	
				Charles "	Son	Unm	15		Ribbon Weaver	do do	
				William "	Son		14		Hand or Power Loom	do do	
				James "	Son		10		Scholar	do do	
				Martha E Kingston	Grand daur			2		do do	
				Elizabeth A Holmes	Grand daur			8 mo		do do	
	Ct 42 - House 7-65		3 U								
82	" " House 1	1		Samuel Ellis	Head	Mar	32		Cordwainer	Cornwall Penzance	
				Elizabeth "	Wife	Mar		35	Boot Closer	Warwickshire Birmingham	
				Thomas "	Son		16		Cordwainer Apprentice	Cornwall Penzance	
				James "	Son		12		Turner at Power Loom	Warwick Birmingham	
	Ct 42 - House 3 & 2		2 U							do Coventry	
83	Ct 42 - House 1	1		George Kirk	Head	Mar	49		Ribbon Weaver	do do	
				Charlotte "	Wife	Mar		49	Silk Winder	do do	
				Henry "	Son		8			do do	
				Joseph Cartwright	Step Son		22		Silk Weaver, Ribbon	do do	
				John "	Step Son		16		Ribbon Weaver Silk	do do	
84	Ct 62 - House 1	1		Henry Aston	Head	Mar	46		Ribbon Weaver	do do	
				Sarah "	Wife	Mar		46	Silk Filler	do do	
				Sarah "	Daur			18	Silk Filler	do do	
				William "	Son		14			do do	
	Total of Houses...	4	5 U	Total of Males and Females...			15	8			

The 1861 census showing Martha living with her grandfather. (RG9/2201/84/14 held at Warwick Record Office)

It seems that these rumours may also have affected an insurance claim at the time of Elizabeth's burial. Elizabeth was a member of the Church General Burial Society with, at the time of her death, an entitlement of £3 15*s*. Did the church think there were immoral goings-on that could affect Elizabeth and father being considered worthy members of the church? A meeting was held to decide how the payment should be made and it was decided that Elizabeth would be 'decently interred'. They paid for a coffin which cost £1 1*s*; a coach and hearse at a cost of 14*s*; the shroud, pall bearers and grave for £1 3*s* 6*d*, and the transportation from the inquest of 7*s* 6*d*. The 7*s* which was left over was given for the welfare of her child.

The child (Martha) was taken to live with Samuel, which is where she is found on the 1861 census. Ten years later it seems the family were unable to care for her anymore, as on the 1871 census she is living in Bristol at the George Muller Orphanage in Ashley Down, a home which housed hundreds of children from all over the country.

SOLVED

CASE SIX 1860

DREADFUL OCCURRENCE IN HILL FIELDS

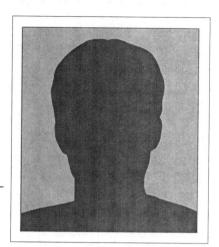

Suspect: Henry Fawson
Age: About 38
Charge: Murder and suicide

On Tuesday last the neighbourhood of Hill Field was thrown into a state of the most painful excitement by the commission of a fearful double crime, under circumstances in the highest degree mysterious and extraordinary. The exact motive for the crime and the circumstances under which it was committed much alike remain forever veiled in impenetrable mystery. The dark tragedy was played out in a little room at the stillest hour of a long, still winter's night ...

Coventry Herald, 10 February 1860

Henry Fawson and Charlotte Sumner were married at St John Baptist, Coventry, on 27 September 1849. He was a butcher living in Fleet Street and she, still a minor, was the daughter of Charles Sumner, a victualler in Bull Ring. It seems that not long after the marriage violent quarrels took place and Charlotte returned to her father's house while Henry went to America, where he stayed for a number of years. Charlotte was certainly living with her father at the time of the 1851 census.

By the late 1850s Henry had returned to Coventry and it seems Charlotte was pleased to see him once more, making every effort to achieve a reconciliation with her husband. It appears that she achieved this, since in September 1859 she moved into Henry's home and butcher's shop in the Hill Fields district of Coventry.

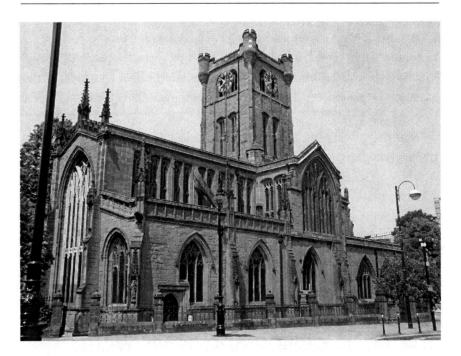

St John's parish church, 2013.

Everyone noticed a change in Henry; they said he was a different man. He was openly affectionate towards Charlotte and was warm and ardent. He bought her new clothes, new furnishings for the house and, during the course of the next five months, no one ever saw or heard them quarrelling. It seems they had become an idyllic couple. But sadly all this was all to change one night in February 1860.

The walls between the neighbouring houses in Junction Street were very thin, with only one set of bricks separated them, and during the early hours of 7 February neighbours heard a faint cry of murder. But because it didn't sound urgent they ignored it. Then almost an hour later they heard a thud, as if something heavy had fallen on the floor.

The next morning the shop wasn't open at the usual time. By ten o'clock George Furnival, who worked for Henry, and the neighbours thought something must be wrong and called the police. Police Constable Russell banged on the door and, when no one answered, he tried to force open the back door but couldn't. It was still locked and bolted from the previous night.

He got a ladder and climbed up to a back bedroom window. Forcing the window open he looked into the room. Nothing seemed amiss but through that room he could see into the front bedroom as the door was open. Within moments he was calling down to the people below, telling them, 'It's a case; I see one dead body!'

Henry was lying on the floor of his bedroom wearing just his shirt. He had two stab wounds in his chest and a wound in his throat. This latter wound had severed his windpipe but hadn't damaged the major arteries. What had killed him was the gunshot wound on the top of his head from which blood was oozing.

Witnesses who went into the room said that the head appeared to have been blown to pieces and 'there was a lot of brains lying on the floor, and that the floor, ceiling and walls were all covered with brains and blood'. A gun lay by Henry's feet, and downstairs on the kitchen table

'the floor, ceiling and walls were all covered with brains and blood'

a bloodstained knife was found. But it was noticed there was no blood in the kitchen or on the stairs.

They found Charlotte lying on the bed with her head hanging over the side. Her throat had been cut.

But who had killed who? Had Henry got out of bed in the middle of the night, gone downstairs, fetched a knife, cut Charlotte's throat then stabbed himself. Then when that hadn't worked had he gone back downstairs to fetch his gun, leaving the knife downstairs. Or had Charlotte stabbed her husband then cut her own throat leaving her husband to shoot himself while in a grief-stricken state. No artificial light would have been needed as the moon was shining so brightly. But from the noises the neighbours had heard there was a gap of forty-five minutes. So what could have been going through Henry's head during that time was something everyone was wondering.

An inquest was held on the Wednesday morning at the Elephant and Castle in Hill Fields, and those who had last seen the couple, or who had

Opposite St John's is the tiny section of Fleet Street which remains today.

heard anything, were called in order for the coroner to try to piece together the evidence.

Sixteen-year-old George Furnival had worked for Henry for seven months. At half past six on the Monday evening Henry had gone out and left George alone with instructions of what was left to do. George finished his work at half past eight and locked the shop up as he left. He told the coroner that he knew Henry had a gun in the house. He kept it by the clock in the kitchen and used it to kill the animals with. It was a double-barrelled shotgun which had been loaded only recently to kill a cow, but only one barrel had been emptied at the time. George said he had never seen the knife before.

Joseph Elton, a publican, went round to the Fawson house at about half past nine that evening for some steak. Henry was now back home and he and Charlotte were sitting by their fire talking. They were discussing moving to a larger house. Elton said Charlotte appeared happy and cheerful but he thought Henry didn't seem in quite such high spirits.

Henry and Charlotte's next-door neighbour from No. 18 Junction Street, a grocer named Thomas Waleman, said he heard faint cries of murder during the night but thought they had come from the street. He said it was about twenty minutes to two and as he lay listening he realised the noises were coming from next door. He woke his wife who got up and lit a candle. But then it all went quiet so they dozed back off to sleep. About an hour later he was aroused by the sound of a heavy thud. This he could tell had come from next door. Mrs Waleman was now nervous so she and her husband sat up until six o'clock in the morning. Soon after this, Thomas went across the road to 'Snape the pork butcher' to voice his concerns. Snape, however, said not to worry and wait to see if the shop was opened at the usual time. If it wasn't then something would have to be done about it.

The neighbour on the other side, John Paul, said he had heard Henry chopping meat sometime during the evening, sometime between nine and ten o'clock. Later in the night he also heard weak moans of murder and had put his ear to the wall. He heard the moans repeated several times so had knocked on the wall and called out, 'Whatever is the matter?' but everything went quiet. He thought perhaps Charlotte wasn't well and was moaning in her sleep.

Henry's sister, Eliza Carter, who lived in Gosford Street, sobbed all the time she was giving evidence. She said her brother had visited her on the Monday evening at about a quarter to nine and stayed about twenty minutes. He had then gone outside to talk to his nephew but had left without going back in the house to say goodbye to her. This she thought was strange. A jury member asked her if there was any history of insanity, or symptoms of madness in the family. She said there wasn't but she had been told that her brother had been ill while living in America.

Dr Goate, the surgeon who examined the bodies, said Charlotte's windpipe had not been injured which was why she had still been able to speak as she lay bleeding to death. The angles of the cuts showed that they could not have been self-inflicted; they were the wrong angle. But her hands were not injured or cut in any way, which showed there had been no struggle. It seemed she was attacked while she was sleeping.

Henry's injuries were self-inflicted. Although it could never be certain what Henry's movements were, it appeared that after cutting Charlotte's throat he had cut his own throat and then stabbed himself. Not having done this sufficiently enough to kill himself he had gone downstairs to fetch his gun. He'd put the knife down on the table, picked the gun up, then went back upstairs to his bedroom and shot himself. As the *Coventry Herald* later described it, '... without, so far as is known, one word of disagreement, the murderer hurried his victim from the sleep of healthy life to the sleep of solemn death; nor did he hesitate to follow her to her untimely tomb.'

Dr Goate concluded his explanation by stating that insanity was usually hereditary and that it was also unusual for it to come on very suddenly;certainly not suddenly enough for that person to commit murder in an instant. It was then mentioned that there was a sister who had been confined to a lunatic asylum four years previously and, although she wasn't there now, she did still have bouts of violence. However, Dr Goate still did not agree that this was sufficient evidence that Henry was also mentally unstable.

After consulting for two hours, the jury brought a verdict which condemned Henry for the wilful murder of Charlotte and *Felo de se* (felon of himself). No agreement was made as to whether it was through insanity or not.

Henry Fawson was buried later that same night in St Peter's churchyard. There was no funeral service. Charlotte, however, was buried on 11 February at the London Road cemetery.

A few weeks later a notice appeared in the *Coventry Herald*:

All persons having any claim or demand against the estate and effects of Henry Fawson late of the City of Coventry, butcher, deceased, are required to send particulars thereof to Mr J.T. Eburne, accountant, Spon Street, Coventry, within seven days from the date hereof, and all persons indebted to his estate are required to pay the amounts thereof to Mr Eburne without delay.

DEATH UNDER SUSPICIOUS CIRCUMSTANCES

Suspect: William Beamish
Age: About 35
Charge: Murder

This case, which has excited more interest in this City than any case within the memory of the oldest inhabitant, has terminated fatally to the prisoner. Throughout the whole of yesterday the excitement was intense, almost painful. It appears that the prisoner confidently anticipated that the verdict would be in his favour. Many persons entertained the same opinion, thinking that there was an important link wanting in the chain of evidence to substantiate the charge. The remarks of the Judge in his charge to the Grand Jury very much favoured this opinion, and made even those who had little doubt of a conviction previously begin to think that it might even turn out to the prisoner's advantage.

Coventry Times, 18 December 1861

William Beamish married Betsey Stokes at the Vicar Lane Chapel in Coventry on 11 August 1849. In 1861 they are living at No. 28 Spencer Street with their three children, William aged 9, Lizzy aged 3 and 1-year-old Emily. Four months later this family would be torn apart by tragedy. Betsey and her children would be stricken down with sickness and diarrhoea and first Emily would die, then Betsey herself would die.

On Wednesday, 14 August William went to work as usual in Mr Hart's factory where he had been working as a weaver for a month, having been forced to give up his own business after what seems to have been

The vast, huge spread of Coventry cemetery today.

financial difficulties. During his breakfast break he went to visit his sister, Emma Harper, but while he was there a boy came to say his family were ill and he was to go home. He went to the factory first to be excused before leaving. Once home, Betsey said they had had their breakfast of coffee and bread then had all been sick. The following day Emily died.

Young William and Lizzy improved as the day went on but Betsey remained unwell, although she did manage to take her baby to the London Road cemetery the following day to be buried.

At the funeral a neighbour noticed how very ill she looked and expressed concern. Betsey returned home and went straight to bed. She was very thirsty and her tongue was extremely red and dry so her husband went to fetch Dr Goate. Betsey also complained to the doctor of pain in her chest and throat and said she couldn't keep anything down. Dr Goate declared she was very unwell and prescribed an aperient. He then continued to visit over the next couple days until she seemed to be getting better.

Her sister-in-law Jane Stokes, who lived close by, had offered to help look after her but Betsey said that 'her husband was very kind to her, and if she only moved her hand would get up and give her anything she might require.'

On 20 August William went round to Dr Goate telling him Betsey had died and asked for a certificate in order to go to the registrar to register the death. Dr Goate issued the certificate giving the cause of death as gastritis. Something he was later to be reprimanded for – having issued the death certificate without seeing the body. However, after thinking about it, Dr Goate decided that perhaps there should be a post-mortem as when he had last seen Betsey she had been improving. The post-mortem didn't show anything in particular, apart from inflammation of the stomach, but as this was consistent with metallic poisoning it was decided that a portion of the stomach, liver and transverse colon should be sent for analysis.

After Betsey had died, Jane Stokes had asked William if it was possible for her to have one of Betsey's outfits. She wanted to pass it on to someone she knew who was in need. William took her upstairs to choose one. While searching in the pockets of the dress a piece of paper fell out. It was addressed to Jane and read:

For Jane Stokes. Dear Sister – if anything happens to me do not let them blame anyone but me for God forgive me I did not know what I was doing but the thought of losing my home and to see how the poor lad was fretting to know what to do for the moment drove me mad for to lose my home I could not bear the disgrace after living respectful so long and do not tell him if you can help it for it will drive him mad Jane see to the little one for he is so fond of Lizzey God Bless and comfort my poor lad. Betsey Beamish, 14th Aug.

This was quite a shock but Jane was also puzzled about the note; she didn't think Betsey could write as she hadn't been to school. But knowing William was a Sunday school teacher and could write, she thought that perhaps he had taught his wife. Although Jane had never heard that he had.

An inquest into Betsey's death was held on Monday, 22 August at the Gloucester Arms, Stoney Stanton Road, but was adjourned for a week awaiting the results of the tests. By the next Monday the case had taken a dramatic turn and hundreds gathered to try to get into the public house to hear the evidence. William had been arrested on suspicion of murdering his wife.

The tests had shown that the stomach contained arsenic. And it had also been discovered that William had gone into a chemist and druggists on Smithfield Street on the Saturday after Betsey had been taken ill, asking for some arsenic. John Bennett, Mr Jenkins apprentice, told William he couldn't have any without the usual witness. He left but was soon back with a witness and signed the appropriate book. Mr Jenkins warned him of the dangers and William said he needed it to kill some rats. He said his wife was ill and he was concerned it was due to rats which he thought he had seen about. Mr Jenkins suggested Battles Vermin Killer but William said he had tried that but it hadn't seemed to work.

Inspector Frederick Payne arrested William at eleven o'clock on the Friday night, 26 August. On searching him he found a packet of poison in his breast pocket. William said it was for the rats. He had mixed some of

'a packet of poison in his breast pocket'

it with oatmeal and strewn it around the peas in his garden. Payne went to the garden with William but couldn't see evidence of any poison having been sprinkled.

The gardener and bailiff of the Harnall Lane gardens were taken to examine Beamish's garden. He said he couldn't find any trace of poison or oatmeal either. And none of the other tenants had ever complained of vermin.

But there was more incriminating evidence. Although friends said William had always been kind and affectionate towards Betsey, this had begun to change in the last eighteen months. It seems William had met another girl by the name of Emma Statham. A neighbour, Sarah Turner, had first seen them together on some grass, some distance from the road, where they obviously thought they wouldn't be spotted. William had his arm around Emma's waist and she had her hand in his.

They were seen again in the Shepherd and Shepherdess on Keresley Road. They were alone in the parlour, holding hands and kissing. Another time they were spotted in Tew's Lane and Emma was heard to say, 'I think somebody is coming.' William had replied that he didn't care. 'He was sworn to have her and do all he could for her,' he had said. They had been seen frequently together in the last three months in his workshop where they thought they couldn't be seen, 'always kissing and messing about'. But unbeknown to them a neighbour's back window overlooked onto the windows of the shop.

Elizabeth Cox of the Rose public house had seen them in there, many times. She said, 'I always thought from their manner and conduct that they were parties courting.'

Emma had been employed by William when he had his own shop and had worked for him for two or three years. But she denied ever being alone with William, apart from when he walked her home at night from the shop, and nothing improper had ever taken place she said. She admitted she had seen him in the public houses referred to but they had never been on their own. She had been there accompanied by other friends and he had just happened to come in.

On the strength of the evidence she was arrested as an accessory.

The note Betsey had supposedly written was also an incriminating factor for William. Her brother, Mark Stokes, said Betsey had never learnt to write. He was also a witness at her wedding and from what he could remember was sure she had only made her mark in the register. However, John Weston, the registrar, said he thought Betsey did write her own name. For some reason, not explained, the registers were never brought to court in evidence.

Joseph Netherclift, a lithographer for the British Museum, was brought from London to examine the handwriting in William's books and the letter. He had a good reputation and had been giving evidence in courts of law for thirty years and said that all the papers and the letter had been written in the same hand.

Everything went against William and the coroner's jury found him guilty of both the murder of his wife and the murder of his baby. After lengthy consultations with the coroner the jury decided that Emma hadn't been involved in the murder and she was discharged. The coroner agreed that although he considered her a girl of bad character there really was no evidence to connect her with the murder.

William appeared at the Warwick Assizes on 17 December 1861 and 'in a firm voice pleaded not guilty to the whole of the charges'. After hearing all the evidence, the judge told the jury that there were two striking points to the case that they must consider. If it had been suicide how likely was it that a woman would administer poison to herself in a way that would also inflict danger to her children. And they also had to consider the way the note had got into her pocket. She had worn that dress for her daughter's funeral so did she put it there on her return home, knowing what she planned and when she was still able to. Or was it William who had put it there as a ploy to shift the evidence away from himself. The jury retired to consider the case and came back to announce a guilty verdict.

When sentencing him to death the judge said that poisoning was the worst form of murder. It was difficult to discern, so when it was discovered, it should be punished accordingly, as in the eyes of the law the guilty party could never be trusted again. He told William, 'You will have what your poor wife – except in the consolation of her own religious spirit – was denied at her last moments, the advice of a Minister of your own persuasion; and I warn you that you might to attend to his adminis-trations as a dying man!' adding that he could expect no mercy, only the mercy of God. William appeared to be extremely shocked by the verdict and clutched the rail tightly to prevent himself from falling. After the sentence had been passed he was only able to make his way from the dock with the help of two of the gaolers.

William Beamish was executed on a scaffold hung over the entrance to the Warwick County Gaol at ten o'clock on 30 December 1861. People started arriving early, some at five o'clock in the morning. (It was a double execution: John Thompson, who had murdered his housekeeper in Birmingham, was also being executed.) Despite the cold, the watchers stood patiently for several hours so as not to lose their places at the front, and as the time for the execution approached they began to get impatient and 'in order to while away the time they swayed about in long waves'.

Once the prisoners were brought out the hangman acted quickly and in no time the two lifeless bodies were hanging side-by-side. 'No sooner had the drop fallen than there was a peculiar convulsive shudder, and the two twisted round facing each other. It would seem that in consequence of Beamish being a much lighter man his neck was not at once dislocated by the fall, as there was a strange tremor of the limbs and body for nearly half-a-minute,' the report described.

William had written a letter to his local chapel minister confessing the crime. He said that when the family had been ill he realised it would be a good cover-up and so went and bought the poison. He put it in Betsey's medicine on the Saturday night:

> To enter into the reason why I did it will do no good; but it was my own wicked heart that led me to do it, and I hope I may be forgiven. Dear Sir there was no particular premeditation, but it was done altogether, as if all my wickedness was contained in the one deed. Oh! What nights of anguish did I suffer. I fell on the bed beside her and would have given my life to have her back, but too late!

He said that he thought that if he had hired a cleverer lawyer he might have been acquitted. Indeed, right up until the judge's summing up he professed to have had hopes of acquittal.

His two children went to visit him before his execution but his little girl did not recognised him in his prison clothes. Reports said that the meeting was so poignant that even the gaolers were close to tears. William left letters for his children, which were sent to them on the day before his execution. He told them to always speak the truth, to stay away from bad company and to avoid drinking too much intoxicating liquor.

Ten years later, in 1871, his son William is living with his aunt and uncle, Isiah and Sarah Stokes at the Rainbow Inn in Cook Street. Just around the corner his sister Lizzie is living at the Freeman Orphan School in Swanwell Terrace. Ten years later she married George John Munton and moved to Birmingham. Hopefully she took her father's advice, as her brother seems to have done. On 2 July 1871 he married Emma Bree at the Well Street chapel and then moved to Aylestone in Leicestershire where in 1881 his occupation is given as greengrocer and Methodist preacher.

MURDER ON GOSFORD STREET

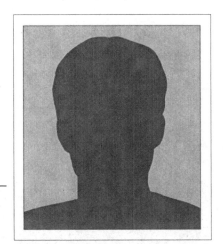

Suspect: Arthur Brown
Age: 18
Charge: Murder

The prisoner, since his apprehension, has behaved with great coolness. His appearance, as his years might be expected to indicate, is that of a mere stripling. The aspect of his face is intelligent, but he wears a somewhat callous look, and does not seem to realise to its full extent the serious nature of his position. While the mother of the unfortunate victim of his passion was giving her evidence in tremulous tones, no trace of emotion was visible on his countenance – his manner, while free from all trace of bravado, was composed and self-possessed, and no one could infer from it that he felt great remorse for his crime.

Coventry Herald, 8 December 1871

John Millward, Arthur Brown, Jane Hewitt and Alice Hancox were four young friends who all worked together at the Leigh Mills in Coventry. Arthur had been given leave of absence for three days from 13 September 1871 as his mother had been ill. When he hadn't returned to work, the overseer, Alfred Saunders, sent someone to Arthur's house to see where he was, but every time someone called round to the house, Arthur wasn't in. Then Saunders heard that Arthur had gone to 'Eaves Place', where the music hall took place. If he had been able to visit the music hall then Arthur should have been able to go to work Saunders had thought. So he suspended him. In the meantime John Millward had been promoted to assistant overseer.

Corner of The Burges and Hales Street, *c.* 1920.

A couple of days later, Arthur met up with Jane and Alice on The Burges. As they walked together to the circus the girls commented on Arthur not being at work and Arthur said he was convinced it was John who had informed on him. 'I know it was Millward. I have had my knife in him for some time, and I shall have my revenge upon him yet,' he told them.

Alfred Saunders was later to say that he had suspended Brown after his failure to return following his consented leave of absence and for no other reason. He said that Millward had never said anything to denounce Brown.

Arthur had also been keeping company with a young woman by the name of Martha Waters but the relationship had recently ended and she had become interested in another young man. Arthur had taken this badly. He had written her a note pretending to be this young man and asked her to meet him. The note was given to her by John Millward at work but he, knowing it was really from Arthur Brown, warned her. He told her to be careful as he knew Arthur had a pistol and that she should take a friend with her to this meeting. In the event, Arthur didn't turn up and she assumed it was probably because he knew she wasn't alone.

Another view of The Burges prior to demolition, *c.* 1920.

Arthur and John were both 18 years old and John lived with his widowed mother at a house in Court 19 along Gosford Street while Arthur lived with his mother, who was separated from his father, at No. 10 Jesson Street. On the opposite side of Gosford Street from the entry to Court 19 was a grocer's shop run by George and Annie Brown.

On 6 December, at half past six in the evening, Annie and their apprentice, Frederick Wimbush, heard a commotion outside. Frederick heard a voice cry out, 'You scamp, I'll have you locked up tomorrow morning!' He, Mrs Brown and a lad named Henry Nibbs, who was in the shop at the time, rushed outside. John Millward was staggering in the road outside the entry of his court. They saw Arthur Brown running away towards Gosford Street Bridge.

John stumbled towards them and as he pulled open his coat they could see a great deal of blood oozing out of a wound in his left side. Mrs Brown told Frederick to take him to the Fox and Vivian inn for some brandy while she went for help. John, however, was too exhausted, so Walter, with the help of others who had come to see what had

Gosford Street today.

happened, carried John into his house. He died a few minutes later. The newspapers, quoting Frederick, wrote that 'with the little life that was left in him he there and then declared that Brown had stabbed him to the heart'.

Police Sergeant Sheasby went off in search of Arthur Brown but he wasn't at his mother's house. Officers also went to search for him at his father's house but he couldn't be found. Investigations eventually led them

'a great deal of blood oozing out'

to a house in Court 2, Chauntry Place, where he had recently taken up lodgings. They were let in by his landlady and found him in bed, but not asleep. When told he was wanted for the stabbing he said, 'I am sorry I did it, but I did it in a passion; he taunted me so.'

A sharp pocketknife of 3¾in in length, with bloodstains on it, was found on the sideboard. Police also found a loaded pistol with a quantity of loose ammunition.

Chauntry Place today.

The surgeon described John's wound as being ¾in long, ¼in wide and 3in deep. The knife had entered between the fifth and sixth ribs, an inch from the sternum or breast bone. The heart had a wound passing through it which had severed the coronary blood vessels. The diaphragm was also pierced and the abdomen and lungs contained a lot of coagulated blood.

A witness, the tailor Henry Carvell, said he had seen Brown standing at the entry where Millward lived. That was about a quarter past six. Carvell said it was very dark but Arthur 'looked at me very hard as I passed, and I looked at him. I have no doubt he was the man.'

Henry Benson, another worker at the mill, had also had a conversation with Brown about his recent dismissal. Benson said that Arthur told him he had had a grudge against John Millward for some time but now it had become worse. He had said, 'I am not coming back at all, for John Millward has gotten me the sack, and I will kill him for it.'

John Millward's funeral took place on 11 December at half past two in the afternoon:

An immense concourse of people assembled to witness and to accompany the procession to the Cemetery. The mourners were the deceased's mother, who was supported by a companion of her late son and two sisters and a brother of the deceased. As might be expected, the mother of the unfortunate young man was quite overcome with emotion, and hardly able to bear up under the weight of excessive grief. The mental distress of the other members of the family was no less painful to witness, and many a sympathetic tear was shed by the bystanders.

While in gaol awaiting trial Brown had written to John's mother:

My dear Mrs Millward – I write to you asking for forgiveness for killing my last companion John. I have repented ever since I done it. I pray night and morning for my sins and also for John and for you, for the Lord to keep you up in your trouble. I have your feelings as well as my own. I did not think what I was doing when I done it, and, if I should get over this, I will think it my duty to do all what lies in my power, and give you as much as I can out of my wages. Forgive me. I think it has not only caused trouble between you and me, but others. Forgive me, I ask you once more, or I shall not rest happy.

The assizes took place at Warwick on Wednesday, 20 December and Mr Bristowe, for the defence, asked that the letter should be read out in court. Supposedly to show Brown wasn't all bad and that the verdict should be one of manslaughter, not murder. In his summing up to the jury he asked them to look at Brown and at his history. His conduct had previously been good. Even directly before the murder he couldn't really have premeditated it. Why stand in the street waiting for Millward to come home where he could be seen. Why not go down the dark alley and wait.

But the prosecution, the Honourable E.C. Leigh, advised the jury that the evidence did point to the murder being premeditated and, therefore, the verdict could not be given as manslaughter. The judge reminded them that the prisoner had said it was done in passion, but there had been witnesses which showed that 'he had been indulging angry and revengeful feelings towards the deceased'.

After consulting for five minutes the jury found him guilty of murder but recommended mercy on account of his youth and previous good character. Nonetheless, the judge assumed the black cap and said that he felt the prisoner had nurtured feelings of revenge for some time so that he considered it was a premeditated and intended act. Moreover, it did seem he was lying in wait that night in order to kill Millward. But in passing the death sentence he said that as the jury had requested mercy he would forward this recommendation to those who could give it.

Arthur Brown cried desperately as he stood between the two warders and as he left the court he was in great distress. His family, who were in the gallery, also sobbed bitterly.

The execution was arranged for Tuesday, 9 January but on the Saturday evening prior to this a messenger arrived from the Home Office with documents showing that Arthur Brown had been given a reprieve and his sentence had been commuted to penal servitude for life. He wrote a letter to his mother: 'My dear mother – it is true, as you think, my earnest prayers have been heard, and my reprieve come. My mind was made up to die on Tuesday next. Though I said nothing, I prayed for courage and strength, and I received it.'

On subsequent census he can be found at Her Majesty's Convict Prison in Portland, Dorset.

CASE NINE   1887

A STRANGE TRAGEDY

Suspect:	Thomas Payne
Age:	36
Charge:	Murder

The prisoner, who is rather under middle height, of spare habit, with sandy whiskers, beard and moustache, dark short hair, rather hollow eyes, thin face, aquiline nose, full forehead, and pallid complexion, was without collar or neck tie, and seemed to be in a perfectly rational mood, answering clearly and distinctly the questions that were put to him. On being placed in the dock he stood in one corner of it, gazing, without any apparent concern, at the bench.

Birmingham Daily Post, 5 August 1887

Thomas Payne married Maria Taylor at All Saint's in Coventry on 14 July 1872, when they were both aged around 21.

In 1881 they were living in Gosford Street and he was a labourer. Also living with them was Maria's 16-year-old sister, Charlotte. By 1887 they had moved to No. 16 Little Park Street, the offices of a firm of solicitors, Messrs Troughton, Lea and Kirby, where they acted as caretaker and housekeeper. Charlotte was still living with them; 'Her services being utilised in the domestic work', was the description used in newspapers.

Charlotte had been a member of the Salvation Army for two years which was said to have changed her character dramatically. Previous to this it had been suspected that she and Thomas were having an affair. She had given birth to a stillborn baby two or three years earlier but would never say who the father was. Maria suspected that it was Thomas

Little Park Street today.

and, when she accused him, he threatened her with a knife. Shortly afterwards Charlotte joined the Salvation Army and, if there had been a relationship, then it was ended. Thomas, perhaps still harbouring feelings for his sister-in-law, showed jealousy to anyone who displayed affection towards her. He became jealous of officers she met at the meetings and began to threaten and abuse one such who lived nearby. He also argued with Charlotte over keeping up a correspondence with Leonard Doy, a lieutenant with the Salvation Army who had previously lived in Coventry but had moved to Fakenham, Norfolk. Later, Leonard was to say that he had only respected her as a sister of the army. That there had been no other relationship between them.

On Sunday, 31 July 1887 Charlotte was about to leave for her Sunday evening service. Thomas, seeing her in her Salvation Army bonnet, became irritated and quarrelled with her. He was so angry that he threatened her, shouting out 'Someone's blood shall fly for this!' He told her, if she carried on wearing the bonnet she could no longer live in his house. Maria asked her to take the bonnet off for her sake but Charlotte said, 'Maria, it's nothing to do with him, and nothing to do with anyone. I have only myself to please.'

Leaving for the Salvation Factory, Thomas followed and asked her to return home. He made such a scene that Charlotte was forced to leave with him. Back at the house, however, she soon realised that her sister wasn't home,

'someone's blood shall fly for this!'

and ran out, fearing to be alone with him. It was only after much persuasion that she returned to the house, on the condition that Maria would also be fetched. As she stepped into the house Thomas locked the door and put the key in his pocket. Charlotte ran through the house to the back door and managed to escape once more. Thomas, in hot pursuit, made a grab for her but only managed to snatch the bonnet from her head. That night she stayed at a friend's house; and so did Maria.

A few days later it seems that Thomas's temper had calmed down. Maria and Charlotte were back in the house and their father came to visit them from Birmingham. It was on Thursday morning, 4 August, that Thomas started to act quite strange.

First he woke his wife saying, 'Get up Maria and see the light shining for the last time.'

Then, when they were all having breakfast, he said, 'Maria, are you going to have your breakfast? It's the last breakfast we shall have together.'

He made other strange statements: 'Maria, if General Booth only knew what will soon happen it would pay him to take all three of us straightway into the Army work' and, 'Maria, if you only knew what you soon will you would consent to anything.'

Charlotte left the breakfast table and took a duster to start cleaning the offices on the first floor while Maria went through to the hall with two buckets. Within minutes she heard a gurgling and muffling sound. Perhaps it was a premonition which told her what was happening because she flung open the front door shouting 'murder!' She next called out 'Charlotte!' six times but had no answer. When Thomas appeared he said, 'Maria, Charlotte's dead; I've murdered her, and it's all ended.'

Amazingly No. 16 Little Park Street still stands today having survived Hitler's bombs.

With this Maria ran out and went straight to the police station. By the time she got there she was in a hysterical state and Inspector Wyatt tried to calm her to find out what was wrong. Shortly afterwards, Thomas followed her in and, quite calmly and rationally, said, 'If you go into Little Park Street you'll see what's the matter.' An officer took him out into the station yard to wait under guard while Inspector Wyatt and Police Constable Spicer went to the offices in Little Park Street. Here they found Charlotte's body.

The surgeon who later examined her body said, 'The gash in the throat commenced about two inches below the left ear and extended to within the same distance of the right ear. The eyes were wide open and the features in repose, the face being free from any expression of agony.'

The evidence showed that Thomas had gone into the clerk's office where she was cleaning, grabbed her from behind then cut her throat. It seemed that Charlotte had tried to get the knife from him as she had several cuts to her hands. One cut was so bad it would have rendered the hand useless. The blood must have poured out from the wound in her throat and she presumably fell to the floor, dying instantly.

At the Warwick Assizes, on Friday, 18 November, Thomas was asked how he would plead and announced, 'I am guilty my Lord.' He said he had had no intention of taking Charlotte's life; it had all been in the heat of the moment. He gesticulated wildly, saying the cause of the crime had been his wife's hatred and unfaithfulness: 'If she has not got a spot in her heart for me, there is a chamber in mine for her.' He said it had been his endeavour to be true to his wife but she had been unfaithful to him and had wanted to go away. If she could have loved properly he should not have been standing there that day. It was she who was her sister's murderer.

As he had pleaded guilty no evidence was produced. It had previously been thought that the defence would have brought in a plea of insanity, owing to an injury Thomas had received in a fall a short time before the murder. However, Thomas insisted he was guilty and that he was ready to die. As such all that was left to do was for the judge, Mr Baron Huddleston, to pass sentence. As he passed the death sentence he told Thomas that he should hold no hope of mercy. The execution was set for Tuesday, 6 December at Warwick Gaol.

In the days leading up to the execution Thomas often spoke of his sorrow for committing the murder, but continued to say that he was ready to die. At times his spirits were low but at other times he was actually quite cheerful. Those who spent time with him in the gaol said the impression they got of him was that it must have been an absolute frenzy that had driven him to commit the crime. A frenzy which had prevented him from controlling his actions. He never made any accusations against his wife as he had in the court room and his gaolers thought that the outburst had been the result of his imagination.

On the Monday afternoon prior to his execution his wife visited him for the one and only time. She was accompanied by his sister and he prayed for her forgiveness.

On the morning of the execution he woke at six o'clock and had breakfast at seven.

Executions were now private affairs and took place within the confines of the gaol. Newspaper reporters were, however, allowed to witness the execution and they were there as Thomas was taken out into the yard. It was five to eight in the morning and he was accompanied by a large group of officials. These included the undersheriff and warders, together with the prison chaplain, the prison governor, the surgeon, the executioner and the Revd G. Sumner, who read a portion of the burial service as they walked. Thomas looked very pale but walked firmly and unassisted. His lengthy beard, which he had worn in the dock, had been cut close to his face. On meeting Berry, the executioner, he shook hands with him saying, 'Good morning. God bless you. I hope to meet you in heaven.'

He was then led to the place of execution. Reports said, 'His pinched and haggard features wore an agonised look.'

As Berry adjusted the rope and put the white cap over the prisoner's head, Thomas spoke in a clear voice, 'God bless her and help her – save her soul. God bless me. God bless my wife. Receive my soul, my Lord, my Jesus.' By the end his voice had risen to a passionate pitch and his hands were tightly clasped.

Death was instantaneous and about twenty people outside the gaol walls watched as the black flag was hoisted to show the execution had taken place. Inside, Berry beckoned to the reporters, who were standing close by, to come and view the body hanging motionless in the pit. They noted that the hands were still clasped.

Within a year Maria had married Henry Molesworth at St Michael's, Coventry, on 7 October 1888. In 1891 she was still living, and acting as caretaker, at No. 16 Little Park Street.

CASE TEN   1906

A DOUBLE MURDER

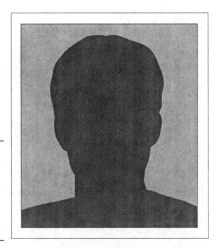

Suspect:	Charles Ernest Robert Taylor
Age:	21
Charge:	Murder

The prisoner, who was in the custody of a warder, stepped smartly into the dock. Quietly dressed in a black suit, his appearance is that of a respectable artisan. He is fairly tall, and the breadth of his shoulders and generally sturdy build indicate great bodily strength. He appeared to be quite unconcerned at what was going on, and it was noticed that once or twice he turned and smiled at someone sitting at the back of the court.

Leamington Spa Courier, 23 March 1906

That prisoner was Charles Ernest Robert Taylor who had been brought before the magistrates at St Mary's Hall, Coventry, for the murder of Richard and Mary Phillips in January 1906. He was aged 21, lived at No. 16 Spencer Street and work as a carpenter.

Richard and Mary were an elderly couple who had lived at Hawthorne Cottage, off the Binley Road, in the Stoke Park estate. They had last been seen on 10 January and a light had been seen in their house at ten o'clock on that evening. Nevertheless, when people had called at their house the following day they received no answer. Richard and Mary seemed to be out.

Three days later there was still no sign of them and still no answer when Daniel Shell, delivering bread, knocked on the door. Looking around he noticed that the pantry window was open. It seemed as if it had been broken open and plates, which had lain on the ledge, had now fallen

St Mary's Hall on Bayley Lane.

into the garden. With the help of a neighbour they managed to enter the house through the broken window.

There was no indication of anything wrong on the lower level so they went upstairs. Blood was splattered everywhere, over the walls and the floors. They found Mary upon the bed with four wounds to her head and Joseph lying on the floor of the bedroom with sixteen wounds, also to the head. Some had been incurred after his death; the culprit obviously making sure his victim was dead.

The police were called and Detective Inspector Imber and Detective Sergeant Basset searched for evidence. The bedroom had been ransacked and drawers left half open. Richard's pockets had been emptied, but Mary still had a purse in the pocket of her dress and a lady's silver watch and gold chain lay on a wicker table in the bedroom. A cash box lay empty with its inside taken out. Downstairs, money amounting to £16 10s was found hidden in a flowerpot in the conservatory and a calendar, sitting on the mantelpiece in the sitting room, still showed the date as 10 January. In the kitchen was a bottle of brandy and a bicycle lamp, which police suspected had been used by the criminal, or criminals, to search the house.

Charles Taylor hadn't gone home on the night of 10 January. His mother had left a lamp burning for him but, when she got up in the morning, she found him sitting in the kitchen warming his hands. She asked why he hadn't been to bed and he said he was sorry but he had broken the pledge and had drunk too much. He had been ashamed and so had gone to his workshop in Jenner Street to sleep.

Binley Road today.

It soon became clear that an incident a few months earlier could be linked with the murder of Richard and Mary. In September 1905, a youth by the name of John Lament had reported that his bicycle had been stolen. Then a month later Charles had sold parts of a bicycle to two people, Thomas Eales and Henry Lester. Through the diligence of the police those parts were recovered and, when put together, were identified as those taken from the stolen bicycle. One part was still missing, however – the lamp. The lamp found in Hawthorn Cottage was therefore shown to John Lament and he identified this too as belonging to his stolen bicycle. Prior to his bicycle having been stolen a wheel had caught in a rut and he had fallen off. The bicycle and the lamp had suffered various dents which were recognisable. When shown to Charles' parents they also recognised it as a lamp which had been in their house and soon suspicions were aroused. It was a great shock for Charles' parents when police informed them where the lamp had been found; in fact, Charles' mother fainted.

Charles Taylor was a distant relative of Richard Phillips and, along with his father Robert, who was also a carpenter, Charles had been asked to make the coffins. Both father and son went to the funeral but Charles refused to help put the bodies into the coffins.

On the morning of 11 January, sometime between four and half past four, Benjamin Taylor (no relation to Charles) had seen two men coming along the Binley Road from the direction of Hawthorn Cottage but on the opposite side of the road to him. When they were nearly opposite him they noticed him across the street and turned, running back to where they had come from. Then they disappeared. The younger of the two men was about 26 years of age, 5ft 7in tall with a slim build and in dark clothes.

Benjamin Taylor went to the Phillips' funeral on 17 January and was sure he saw that man again so alerted the police.

Also on 11 January, at around four o'clock in the morning, John Boneham, a haulier, went out to his stables on the Walsgrave Road. In the next field there was a footpath which connected the Wallsgrave and Binley roads and here he saw a man coming along the footpath towards Wallsgrave Road. He had his head bent down and was walking fast. It appeared that he had something under his coat in his right hand. John said good morning and the man, according to John, 'roughly returned the salutation'. He similarly described the man as aged about 26, 5ft 7in tall, slim build, clean shaven and wearing a dark coat and cap.

Both Benjamin Taylor and John Boneham picked Charles out of a line-up of six or seven men at the police station.

On the day before the murder Charles was said to have acted strangely. In the afternoon he had gone into a shop owned by Thomas Eales and fired a revolver; in 'tomfoolery' he had said. Then he went into an inn on the Stoney Stanton Road with a friend and ordered two drinks offering to pay for them with ten farthings and two half-pennies.

Amos Statham, the innkeeper, thought it strange that someone should have that amount of farthings so refused to accept them, believing they could be fake. Charles started to argue with him, then pushing his coat

Another part of Little Park Street today.

tails to one side and revealing the butt of a revolver in his pocket, said he was not hard-up and could get £3 for this article. Amos and another man managed to take the revolver away from him and Charles was asked to leave. He then went on to the Woolpack inn and played darts with William Scott. Witnesses here reported that he soon appeared to be in a very drunken state and the landlord, William Hanson, said Charles did seem different to how he normally was. He was excited and wild, but Hanson didn't think Charles was drunk. From there Charles went to Charles Jordan's house for his supper, leaving at half past ten saying he was going to a club in Little Park Street.

Medical examinations on the bodies suggested the wounds had been inflicted with a curved instrument. In September 1905 Charles Taylor had asked Thomas Eales to make him two iron jemmies (short crowbars), 18in long, flattened broad and bent at each end. A couple of months later he'd taken one back and asked that it be made into an ordinary chisel.

After the murder the curved jemmy had disappeared and Charles refused to say where it was.

Charles also seemed to be having financial problems. At his house police had found a county court summons for money he owed. His father said his son had been in difficulties for some time and he had lent him £10 to cover the initial expenses of starting his business up as a builder. Apparently someone he had worked with once said to him, 'Why don't you try your hand at burgling?' Charles had then picked up a chisel and showed how he would open windows with it.

Charles' clothes were sent to Dr Bostock Hill for examination. He said there was no trace of blood on any of them, nor any indication of attempts having been made to remove any bloodstains. Then police searched Charles' workshop and other relevant places to find evidence that he had burnt any clothes. No ashes were found so it couldn't be proved that he had destroyed his bloodstained clothing from that night.

There was also the question as to whether a second man was involved, especially since two men had been seen by Benjamin Taylor on that night. On the way to Warwick Gaol, Charles himself had said, 'I am not going to give anyone away, as I am single; the other is a married man with five children. If I suffer he will thank me for it someday. I expect some kind friend will give me away, and I shall get slung for it.'

Charles pleaded not guilty in front of the magistrates and Mr Masser, his defence lawyer, said there was no proof the couple had been murdered that first night. It could have happened anytime between the 10th and the 14th. Perhaps they had been away and only just returned; which would explain why the money had been hidden in a flowerpot and the door locked. Moreover, the wounds inflicted on the victims would have meant blood would have been found somewhere on Charles' clothes. After all it was splashed all over the walls. The lamp was of no significance at all. Why would Charles have put it down in a corner of the house and then left it. It may have belonged to the couple themselves. It wasn't a rare type and could have been purchased in any second-hand shop.

Despite the efforts of his defence lawyer, the Bench decided, after consulting for some twenty minutes, that Charles should be sent for trial at the Warwick Assizes.

The Summer Assizes commenced on Monday, 23 July and the trial lasted four days. Many additional witnesses were called to give evidence. Neighbours described their last sightings of Richard and Mary Phillips. Mary Jane Cotton said she had seen a light moving about in the conservatory on that first night, like someone was looking for something. A young relative who visited regularly said he didn't remember ever having seen the bicycle lamp before. Percy William who did occasional work for them said he had never seen the lamp either.

Witnesses who had done business with Charles gave him unfavourable references by saying they had not been paid or that he hadn't gone back to pay for and collect the goods he had ordered.

The prosecution had done a good job but the defence did a better one, showing that a lot of the evidence was circumstantial. The judge, Lord Coleridge, explained that circumstantial evidence 'amounts to evidence which gives rise to nothing more than the barest suspicion, or it may, on the other hand, afford grounds for conclusive proof'. He likened it to a net. Small holes still prevented a means of escape, but a large hole made the whole net worthless. He then left the jury to decide for themselves and they took just half an hour to find Charles not guilty.

He showed no emotion when the verdict was read out, but his mother burst into tears. During the trial he had been very self-assured. He stuck by all the previous statements he had made and even when the prosecution asked him if he had ever been arrested he answered, 'I have never been arrested; I have only been detained on suspicion.'

But this wasn't the end of the matter for Charles. A few months later, on 7 December, he appeared at the Winter Assizes charged with the theft of the bicycle and for house burglary. The house in question was his next-door neighbour's, Joseph Wilson. A chain, which had been stolen in the burglary, had been found in Charles' bedroom cupboard. This time Charles was found guilty and was sentenced to fourteen years penal servitude.

A petition was forwarded to the Home Secretary by Mr Masser, asking for a pardon or for the sentence to be reduced on the grounds of it being too excessive for the crime Charles had been tried for. But newspapers reported that less than 100 signatures appeared on the memorial that was attached to the petition. Two months later the reply came back saying that, having looked at the case, the Home Secretary wasn't able to consider a reduction in sentence. In March Charles was taken from Warwick Gaol to Portland Prison in Dorset. He was said to be in good health.

However, it transpired that he didn't complete the whole sentence and was given a ticket of leave in June 1914. Then, on 13 June, he walked into a police station in London's East End, soaking wet, saying, 'I have been in the water. I walked in. I am tired of my life.' He said he had no friends and was very depressed. As a result he was handed over to the Church Army Home.

The First World War saw him in the army where he was sent to France. Here he received shellshock and spent three months in hospital followed by two months in the Hatton Asylum near Warwick. Charles seemed to have recovered and perhaps even found happiness in 1918 when he married Margaret Knibbs in Northampton and made his home at No. 23 Park Street Northampton. But was he still tortured by the deaths of Richard and Mary Phillips, or was it just the aftereffects of the war?

One Sunday afternoon, in April 1922, a man was walking his dog in Gibbet's Hill Woods near Coventry, once a hanging place for eight-eenth-century criminals. Here he found a body hanging from the branch of a tree, 18in high. It was Charles Taylor. A card found on the body read, 'God bless my dear wife.'

His wife said he had left home on the Friday afternoon saying he was going out on his bicycle and she hadn't seen him since. His father, Robert, who still lived in Spencer Street, said he had last seen his son a few days earlier, on 5 April. Robert said that Charles regularly suffered from bouts of depression, revealing that, 'though good in health, his spirits had broken'. On the Friday evening he had heard his letterbox rattle and thought someone was having a joke so didn't go straight to it. Later he found an old rag containing his son's watch and 1s 8½d. A note also lay on the floor which read, 'Dear mother and father. Cheer up and forgive me. Don't forget poor Maggie. Love to all, yours C.E.R. Taylor.'

Robert went to the police to report it then waited all night for news. The murder wasn't mentioned during the inquest but, of course, the *Coventry Herald* added the story to their report to make it more sensational. Was there a reason for Charles going to Gibbet's Hill, a significance that he knew he had committed murder and should have been hanged? No one was ever found for the murder and Charles took the truth with him.

CASE ELEVEN   1908

MURDER IN THE BAKERY

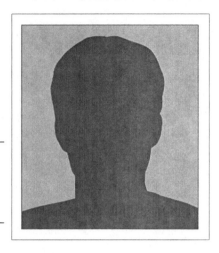

Suspect:	Henry Parker
Age:	31
Charge:	Murder

In accordance with the precedent which has obtained in late years, the execution was strictly private, and, consequently, few particulars are available beyond official information, that the death sentence has been duly carried out. A notice to this effect was posted outside the prison gates shortly after 8 o'clock on Tuesday morning, and at the same time the tolling of the bell at St Mary's church informed the residents of the County town that the condemned man had paid the full penalty of the law. It was a gloomy morning, and not more than a dozen people were within the vicinity of the prison gates at the time of the execution.

Leamington Spa Courier, 18 December 1908

At the Coventry police court on 13 August 1902, Harry Taylor Parker was bound over for six months for assaulting his wife of two months. Sarah Ann Hunt, aged 25, had married Harry, also aged 25, at St Mark's church in Coventry on 2 June 1902. They had been neighbours; Harry living at No. 84 Cromwell Street, and Sarah at No. 45. Now, two months later, Sarah was back home living with her mother.

Harry was accused of punching his wife several times two weeks earlier. He had been in a bad mood all week and on the day of the assault he had thrown his dinner into the fire. Sarah had run round to her mother's house then stayed there. Harry said she had 'upbraided him' with being out of work and he had only given her a slight tap on the hand. He said that,

Cromwell Street today.

'the least little word that is said, all her relatives come and interfere'. He also accused her father of having threatened him, saying he would put him on the fire. Sarah told the Bench that it was Harry's temper which caused the trouble and she didn't want to live with him anymore.

Four months later, on 8 December, Harry Parker was again in front of the magistrates at the police court. He had now moved to No. 41 Leicester Street and it seems his wife had not gone back to live with him. She worked for Thomas Mead, a baker, at No. 303 Stoney Stanton Road. One morning in that early December Harry went into Mead's shop and said to him, 'I have brought you my address.' Mead said he didn't want his address he just wanted Parker to pay him the money he owed. Parker then accused Thomas Mead of harbouring his wife and threw a clod of earth at his head. Harry denied throwing the earth, saying that Thomas Mead had just 'got on to him about a small bill' which Mrs Parker owed.

Harry Parker was fined 5s plus costs or seven days imprisonment. He chose to go to prison for seven days.

Stoney Stanton Road today.

Thomas Mead only saw Harry Parker again once after that but, in November 1908, he was going to see him for a third time when he, Mead, gave evidence in another trial against Parker, this time at the Warwick Assizes.

Sometime in 1904 Thomas Mead took 56-year-old Thomas Tomkins into his employment. Tomkins was a quiet man who, according to his wife, never quarrelled with anyone. But he had, at some time, annoyed Harry Parker who, by August 1908, bore a grudge against him.

'There was blood coming from his ear'

At five o'clock on the morning of 26 August 1908, Tomkins went into the bakery at the usual time to start baking the bread for that morning. He was found two and a half hours later by his employer lying on the floor in a semi-conscious state. An hour later he was dead.

Thomas Mead had gone into the bakery around about a quarter to eight and found Tomkins lying on the floor with his hands covered in dough.

Mead tried to lift him but Tomkins muttered something and put his hands to his head. There was blood coming from his ear and his clothes had bloodstains over them. Mead called for a doctor but it was too late.

Detective Sergeant Cox, who came to investigate, found bloodstains on both the floor and the weighing machine. Following the trail of bloodstains onto the grass outside, he found an old oak post which had projecting nails in it. Dr Soden said the fatal wound was caused by one of these projecting nails entering the skull.

A local man named Samuel Clark had an occupation not heard of today; he went around 'knocking people up to go to work', i.e making sure they were awake each morning ready for their working day ahead. One of those he visited on his rounds was Parker's mother at her house at No. 21 Cromwell Street. At twenty past five in the morning he saw her talking to her son Harry near the house and then, later in the morning at around ten o'clock, he saw Harry Parker leaning on the parapet of a bridge 'in a very melancholy state'. When he was on his way to work at five o'clock, another witness, Edward Slack, had seen Harry going towards the bakery.

The bridge on Stoney Stanton Road, just around the corner from Cromwell Street today.

Inspector Basset was sent to arrest Harry and found him at his home in Cromwell Street. When arrested, Parker said, 'I went there with the intention of settling him. If I had known that he was not done for before I left I should have finished him before going away.' He added that he was sorry he hadn't done the other man (meaning Thomas Mead) and made a clean job of it.

In his statement he described how he had slept under some trees and then, at five o'clock, had gone to the bake house. He had been sitting on some bricks outside when Tomkins saw him and told Harry to leave. As Tomkins turned to go inside Harry had picked up the post and hit him on the head with it. He admitted he had held a grudge against Tomkins for some time and as he was out of work he had lost his temper.

At Harry's trial at the Warwick Assizes on 24 November, the defence lawyer, Mr Sandland, told the jury that in cases of murder special care should be taken when sifting through the evidence. When Harry had picked up the weapon had he just intended to cause grievous bodily harm? The jury had to be satisfied that there was intent to murder before convicting. He argued that if Harry had intended murder he would have used a more deadly weapon than a piece of wood. It had just been unfortunate that there were nails in that piece of wood. Sandland added that Harry's statement to the police was just bravado. At the end of the session Mr Justice Sutton reminded the jury to consider all the circumstances and it took them nearly two hours to decide that Harry was guilty of murder.

Throughout the trial Harry Parker had appeared quite unmoved. But, during the first few days afterwards, he became more emotional, knowing he was facing the death sentence.

A petition to the Home Office was prepared by his solicitors, which read:

Your petitioners are of the opinion that the condemned man is of weak intellect and character, and not able to discriminate between right and wrong. He was known to be of an excitable temperament, and in our opinion is not legally responsible for his actions. We also desire to bring before your notice the circumstances of the crime, and say that there is considerable doubt whether the condemned man intended to commit murder.

After reading the details of the case the Home Secretary did not grant a reprieve and Harry Parker was executed on 15 December 1908 at Warwick Gaol. The witnesses to the execution were the governor (Mr E.F. Cavendish), the undersheriff (Mr R.C. Heath), the prison surgeon (Dr Hubert Tibbits), the acting chaplain (Revd Duncan Day) and other prison officials. The hangman was Pierrepoint – from the well-known family of executioners.

CASE TWELVE 1910

POISON IN HIS MOTHER'S DRINK

Suspect: John White
Age: 50
Charge: Attempted murder

Arthur Stokes, who carried the news of Mrs White's death to her son, said that on hearing it prisoner fell down. Witness noticed that he fell 'a knee at a time, and put one hand at the back of him.' He did not assist the prisoner to get up, as he considered it pretence.

Leamington Spa Courier, 4 March 1910

Seventy-eight-year-old Mary Ann White lived alone at No. 50 Howard Street, Coventry, and her only son John lived at Iota House, No. 50 Arden Street, Earlsdon. He visited his mother often. These visits were not, however, appreciated by Mary who wanted her son to stop calling in on her and had told him so. She had also told neighbours she was frightened of him. John had started to buy laudanum for his mother's stomach pains, delivering it to her on his regular visits, but she threw it away telling her friends that 'she would have no more of the stuff; he has put something in it perhaps'.

Meanwhile, John had been telling people that he would be better off when his mother died. He had also started saying that she was unwell. Even more incriminating was the fact that John had taken her will as collateral for money he wanted to borrow, saying that he soon have enough money to pay a loan back. He was an only child and Mary had left everything to him in her will.

Howard Street today.

On 9 January 1910, John went to his mother's house at four o'clock in the afternoon and stayed there until a quarter past seven, despite her having said she didn't want to see him. Usually she spent the evening sitting with a neighbour, Mrs Lathbury, but on that evening Mary didn't arrive. After waiting a while Mrs Lathbury went round to see if Mary was all right, taking another neighbour with her. The house was in darkness but the front door was open. As they entered they could see that Mary was sitting on her sofa but there was no answer when they spoke to her. It was then they realised she was dead. At the same time they spotted a glass of liquid on the table at the side of her. The police were sent for and Arthur Stokes went to fetch John.

When John arrived it was noticed that he was wearing his father's watch and chain, which his mother normally kept in one of her drawers. The police asked him if he knew what the liquid was. He smelt it and said, 'I know what it is. It is cyanide of potassium. I use it for hardening my tools.' He said he had recently bought some and left it in the cupboard at his mother's house. But when they looked the police could find no such substance in the cupboard.

'I know what it is. It is cyanide of potassium.'

By 17 January John had proved his mother's will in the Birmingham Probate Court and the effects amounted to £198 5s 1d. John had got what he wanted. But suspicions were aroused.

After a long investigation, during which the doctors tried to find the cause of Mary's death, the coroner's inquest eventually took place on 26 January. At the end of the session the coroner's jury gave a verdict of wilful murder. John was immediately taken into custody by the police before he had chance to leave the court.

Arden Street, 2013; No. 50 would have been at the top of the road on the left.

At the Birmingham Assizes in March 1910, the case took a dramatic turn and the indictment of wilful murder was remarkably changed to attempted murder. Experts said cyanide potassium was of no use when hardening tools. So why would John have bought it? Questions were also asked as to why he kept it at his mother's house. The glass of liquid, a type of lemonade known as nectar, only contained two grains of the cyanide potassium, which was not enough to kill someone, and there was no evidence that Mary had drunk any of the liquid. Certainly, there was no sign of poison in the stomach at the post-mortem. The tests showed that she was a healthy woman and the cause of death could only be syncope (dropping down dead). In those days it was also referred to as having 'died of fright'. In other words it was thought that Mary had been so frightened when she smelt and tasted the poison in her drink, upon taking a first tiny sip, that it had killed her. It was shown that there was enough poison in the drink to make the person aware that something was wrong.

A friend of John's, a man only referred to as Carden, was brought forward as a witness. He said that sometime during the week, in-between Christmas and the New Year, John had produced a small substance which resembled sugar candy and was the size of a marble. He had said that an amount the size of a pin's head, put into water, would be enough to poison someone.

The prosecution, therefore, put forward the theory that John White had given his mother the drink so he was, in effect, responsible for her death. John denied this, saying that as he had put it in her cupboard his mother must have put it in her drink thinking it was sugar. Cross-examination revealed to the court that there had been no proof of the poison ever being in her cupboard. So had John really left it there or had he just said that in order to appear to be innocent?

In his summing up, Mr Justice Darling said he felt that, because of the quantity of poison, it may have been the beginnings of an attempt, by John, to poison his mother slowly over a period of time. He put it to the jury that, although Mrs White did not die from poisoning, it was possible that she could have died from fright at the thought she was being poisoned. As a result John was found guilty of attempted murder and so, the case having taken its dramatic turn, he escaped the death sentence. Mr Justice Darling sentenced him to penal servitude for life. The newspapers reported with relish the fact that this was the first time anyone had been convicted of actually frightening someone to death.

John appealed against the sentence and this appeal was heard over a period of three days on 22 April, 25 April and 2 May 1910. Mr Maddocks, acting for John White, said that the sentence imposed on John was unjustifiable by law. He argued that the judge had no power to impose a sentence on John since the accused had been tried under the wrong offence. Maddocks further contended that John should have been tried under the charge of attempting to poison the deceased with intent to murder her (Section 14 of the Offences Against the Person Act, 1861). However, he was initially tried for murder and, therefore, should have been found not guilty.

Maddocks went on to say that even on the assumption that John had put the poison in the glass with the intention of doing this several times, believing that this would have the cumulative effect of eventually causing death, this did not amount to an attempt of murder as he wasn't intending to kill his mother with that one dose. It may be that he would have changed his mind before giving her enough doses to bring about her death.

Roland Adkins for the Crown Prosecution read a piece from Stephen's *A Digest of the Criminal Law*:

An attempt to commit a crime is an act done with intent to commit that crime, and forming part of a series of acts which would constitute its actual commission if it were not interrupted. The point at which such a series of acts begins cannot be defined; but depends upon the circumstances of each particular case.

Adkins argued that this particular case came well within that definition and actually putting the poison in the glass went beyond the act of preparation.

Maddocks now stood in reply. He said that John was appealing to the conviction on several accounts. Firstly that there was no reasonable evidence on which to convict him and there was no evidence to show his mother had taken any of the poison. That death seemed to have been caused by syncope or heart failure due to fright. That the quantity of poison was not enough to kill her. That the poison had been put in her cupboard and she may have taken it from there herself. Maddock also referred to the evidence of Carden – the substance he had been shown and the conversation. This showed that John knew what it was and how to use it so the jury of the assizes, on hearing this, and on suggestions made by the judge, would have come to the conclusion that John was attempting to murder his mother. But even so the sentence for attempted murder was only two years imprisonment, not life.

Despite the pleas made on behalf of John White the appeal court dismissed the appeal and John was sent to the Portland Prison in Weymouth.

THE STOKE HEATH TRAGEDY

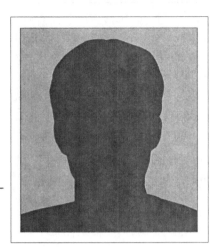

Suspect:	Howard Ball
Age:	50
Charge:	Murder

'Put up Howard Ball,' said the Clerk of Arraign at the Assizes on Tuesday morning, and the middle-aged, tall, and slightly-built man, who was accused of the murder of James Rice, at Wyken, on September 29th last, stepped into the dock. It was the opening statement of the concluding stage of the most sensational drama which has occurred in the Coventry area for some considerable time. Ball appeared as composed as he had done on previous occasions, and had the appearance of a man who had groomed himself as carefully as possible before his trial.

Coventry Times, 22 November 1924

James Rice lived at No. 30 Gun Lane, Stoke Heath, Coventry, in a three-bedroomed house, and rented rooms in the house to two other families. Howard Ball, a labourer aged 50, his wife Sophie, aged 37, and their nine children lived in one of these rooms, seven sleeping in one bed. An elderly couple, William and Agnes Weston, lived in the other room. Agnes acted as the housekeeper and also looked after James' three children who were aged 9, 8 and 5 years old.

Rice, aged 42, was a widower and worked as a fitter at the Dunlop Rim and Wheel Company in Holbrook Lane and it seems that in October 1923 he started taking an interest in Sophie Ball. Six months later it was drawn to Howard's attention and he became convinced the interest was

Gun Lane today.

reciprocated and that his wife was having an affair with James Rice. However, when Ball confronted him, Rice said to him, 'I do not want your wife; I have women of my own, and I do not want you dogging me about.' Why Howard did not find somewhere else for the family to live under these circumstances is not known. Perhaps it was due to the difficulties of the times, even the prosecutor at the assizes said this was one of the tragedies of the case. In any event it is clear that in September 1924 the family were still living in Rice's house and Howard had been out of work for six months.

On 27 September Howard purchased a revolver and six cartridges.

Two days later, on the Monday afternoon, Sophie, carrying her baby of only a few weeks old, went for a walk in the fields around Blackberry Lane. Here she met James Rice. Unbeknown to Sophie, Howard had followed her and saw Rice with his arm around his wife's waist. Albert Walton, who was only a few yards away, heard a heated argument then two gunshots. He saw Rice fall to the ground then, as he tried to struggle to his feet, three more shots rang out and Rice fell back dead.

'Good God man, what have you done that for?' Walton asked.

'The man has spoilt my wife and spoilt my life as well. He has been threatening to shoot me but I have caught him first,' Ball told him.

'What do you mean to do about it now?' Walton asked. Ball was walking away but then turned and said he was going to fetch the police and a doctor.

'Good God man, what have you done that for?'

He did indeed go to a doctor's surgery saying he had knocked a man down and told the doctor where, but then he had disappeared.

After a search of twenty-four hours Howard Ball was found and arrested in Birmingham. He said he had not meant to kill James Rice, just frighten him, and he hadn't realised he had killed him until he read about it in the newspaper. He had gone to Birmingham to get himself some new clothes for any appearances he would need to make before the magistrates. Then he was going to give himself up.

The inquest into the murder opened with the coroner, Mr C.W. Iliffe, condemning the condition of the mortuary in Foleshill which the body had been taken to. The doctor, Dr C.E. Rice (no relation to James Rice), said it was so bad he had been unable to perform a proper post-mortem examination. The mortuary was described as:

> Nothing more or less than an outhouse, its whitewashed bricked walls in filthy condition, and large areas of discoloration where the damp has come through. It is lit by two frosted windows in the roof, of which one large pane is missing, which means that rain is able to pour through upon the contents of the shed.

At the inquest Mrs Weston, Rice's housekeeper, said she had never seen anything which would point to an affair; but that she had noticed James and Sophie 'had been chatty to one another', and she had heard Howard Ball complain about it on several occasions. Both James and Howard would often threaten each other over it.

On the afternoon of the murder James Rice had gone out after his dinner asking Mrs Weston to look after his children and give them breakfast if he wasn't back in the morning. This had surprised her as he had never said anything of the like before. Twenty minutes later Sophie had started dressing her baby in the kitchen saying she was going out. Howard had said he would follow her but first went out to the back of the house. While he was gone, Sophie left saying, 'When Harry comes in tell him I have gone to Mason's to get some butter for tea.' When Howard returned and was told this he was very upset and had said, 'I knew the ____ meant to do me one.' He went out to catch her but, not seeing her, went back into the house and upstairs. He was only up there for a very short time before coming down, saying, 'If I catch them together you will never see Jimmy alive again.'

Twenty minutes later he was back again, saying, 'I've seen them, they are down the fields like a courting couple, with his arm round the missus' waist, and the baby on the other, but I've done him in. Now I am going to the doctor and to the police.'

Sophie Ball, dressed in a full mourning outfit, denied there was any relationship between her and James Rice. Her story contradicted what Mrs Weston had told the court in so far as she said that on that afternoon she had gone out to register the baby's birth. She said she had intended to walk across the fields to Stoney Stanton Road then she had met James Rice by a stile on the Blackberry Lane and he was very drunk. He had said he wanted to go with her but she had told him to go home, knowing her husband intended following her. He would not and had started to walk across the field with her. When she turned round she saw her husband following them. She knew James had got his arm around her waist but it was just to steady himself, as he was so drunk. Howard had showed his wife the gun he had and Rice had walked towards Howard as if he was about to strike him. It was then that Howard had fired the gun. He then ran away and Sophie had rushed to Police Constable Jones' house.

The coroner asked Sophie why the baby's bottle had been found in James' pocket. She said he had taken it off her a few moments before. Albert Walton said she had tried to retrieve the bottle but he had stopped her from touching the body until the police arrived.

Blackberry Lane today.

Dr Rice said that when Howard had appeared in his surgery, he had only admitted to assaulting Rice and so the doctor had been expecting to find someone injured through a scrap. It was with surprise, therefore, that he found Rice had been shot and was dead. He described a wound on the left side of the head and another at the front. A small amount of brain substance was protruding from the front wound, with blood coming from the ear and the nose. When he examined the body later he had also found gunshot wounds in the abdomen.

The revolver was found where Howard said he had thrown it, 'over a hedge in Old Allesley Road'. He was charged with wilful murder and sent to be tried at the next Warwick Assizes in November.

Here, the prosecution, Mr Maurice Healey, described the case as 'a modern eternal triangle', and described James Rice as 'a man who took a certain amount of drink, who did not control himself as he ought to, apparently in some ways a passionate man.' Furthermore, he told the jury he could see no evidence that Ball had fired the shots in self-defence.

In front of the judge and jury Mrs Weston now told how she had seen Sophie and James winking at each other and that she had seen him kiss her once; that things had become so bad that Howard had changed his shifts at Armstrong Sideley from nights to days so he could stay with his wife during the night. Then, in March 1924, he had given up his job completely. When Sophie had left the house that afternoon she seemed to purposely do it while her husband was not there. Mrs Weston also admitted that Rice was not a 'good man morally'; that he often brought women back to the house.

The jury were out for thirty-five minutes, during which time they were instructed to decide if they agreed with the prosecution and, therefore, a verdict of murder; with the defence and, therefore, a verdict of justifiable homicide; or with the judge, who recommended a sentence of manslaughter. They returned to pronounce the verdict of wilful murder, but said that, in view of the circumstances as to the prisoner having suffered at the hands of Rice, they would like to recommend him to mercy. Mr Thomas Hollis Walker, KC said he would convey this to the proper quarter and then passed the death sentence.

Broadgate, looking north with the old mills prominent in the background, *c.* 1930.

Howard Ball seemed unmoved by the verdict but, when asked if he had anything to say as to why sentence shouldn't be passed, his voice was weak as he said, 'I didn't do it with any intent Sir.' He then remained calm as the death sentence was read out and, responding to the tap on his shoulder by a warder, quickly turned and left the dock. His request to see his wife was granted.

At the criminal appeal court on 8 December, Ball's counsel described the appalling conditions in which the parties involved in the case lived. He said that Rice was a powerful man with a violent temper and Ball a small and weak man, who was sober and respectable. The counsel continued to explain that, after almost a year of provocation and aggravated by Rice's conduct towards Mrs Ball, he had been finally tipped over the edge. The appeal court quashed the death sentence and the charge of murder to one of manslaughter, with the lesser sentence of seven years penal servitude.

If you enjoyed this book, you may also be interested in ...

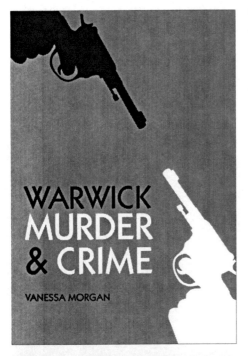

Warwick Murder & Crime
VANESSA MORGAN

Discover the shadier side of Warwick's history with this collection of true-life crimes from the town's past. Cases featured here include a daring robbery at a country house in 1846, the brutal murder of a woman in 1819, and the drowning of a wife by her husband in 1870. Vanessa Morgan's well-illustrated and enthralling text will appeal to everyone interested in true crime and the history of the town.

978-0-7524-8760-1

Murder & Crime Birmingham
VANESSA MORGAN

This chilling collection brings together true-life historical murders that shocked not only the city but frequently made headline news throughout the country. Cases feature riots in 1791, a bank robbery in 1844 and an arson attack in 1912. Murder most foul raises its ugly head; John Thompson stabbed his common-law wife in a fit of drunken jealousy in 1861, and Mary Albion is murdered in her bed when a robbery went wrong in 1898.

978-0-7524-7153-2

Visit our website and discover thousands of other History Press books.

www.thehistorypress.co.uk

Lightning Source UK Ltd.
Milton Keynes UK
UKOW04f0415260314

228801UK00002B/7/P